WHEN SPIRITS VISIT

A COLLECTION OF STORIES
BY
INDIGENOUS WRITERS

Compiled and Edited by
MariJo Moore

rENEGADE pLANETS pUBLISHING
Asheville, NC, USA

Also By MariJo Moore

Returning To the Homeland:
Cherokee Poetry and Short Stories
Crow Quotes
Tree Quotes
Desert Quotes
Bear Quotes
Woestijnwoorden (Desert Words)
Bilingual: Dutch and English
Spirit Voices of Bones
Red Woman with Backward Eyes and Other Stories
The Diamond Doorknob
When the Dead Dream
Confessions of a Madwoman
The Cherokee Little People
The First Fire
The Iceman
The Boy With A Tree Growing From His Ear and Other Stories
A Book of Spiritual Wisdom for all days
A Book of Ceremonies and Spiritual Energies Thereof
Feeding the Ancient Fires: A Collection of Writings by
North Carolina American Indians (editor)
Genocide of the Mind: New Native Writings (editor)
Eating Fire, Tasting Blood: Breaking the Great Silence of
the American Indian Holocaust (editor)
Birthed From Scorched Hearts: Women Respond to War
(editor)
Unraveling the Spreading Cloth of Time:
Indigenous Thoughts Concerning the Universe (editor)

When Spirits Visit

A Collection of Stories
by Indigenous Writers

rENEGADE pLANETS pUBLISHING
Asheville, NC
www.marijomoore.com

First Edition, March 2016
Compilation copyright MariJo Moore

Library of Congress Control Number: 2016930329
ISBN: ISBN-13: 978-1523299713
ISBN-10: 1523299711

Layout, cover and interior design by FireflyInx.com
Cover art: "When Spirits Visit" ©2015
MariJo Moore, mixed media collage
Printed in the USA

Contents

Dedicated to all who know they know...
and those who are beginning to believe...

INTRODUCTION

The stories in this collection all center on spiritual visitation – animal, bird, and people. Some are fiction, some non-fiction, and some faction. I will leave discernment to each reader.

To reiterate what I wrote in *A Book of Spiritual Wisdom –for all days*, which was published several years ago:

"The universe is complex, of this there is no doubt. However, there are natural and spiritual laws that remain true, regardless of who experiences them. This is not to say that humans hold all the answers to the mysteries of the world; this is not possible at this stage of the human race. But many of us do believe in the mysteries of the universe, even if they cannot be "proved" mathematically or scientifically. There are spirit beings who help us, who guide us, and there are spirit beings who can confuse us as well. Spirit beings are all around us at any given moment. These spirits have their work to do in helping us, so they need us as much as we need them."

When Spirits Visit contains writings involving spiritual ancestors, guides, messengers, irritants, and dream gifters. I am very pleased with this collection, and I thank all the writers for sharing their words.

I offer a special expression of gratitude to those who helped in funding this publication:

Jennifer Manning, Wendy Sheridan Stephens (who was also generous enough to be an "outside" reader), Marie R. Nigro, Menoukha R. Case, Lee Karalis, Suzanne Z. Murphy, Susan Deer Cloud, Gabriel Horn and Amy Krout-Horn.

And continuing thanks to Kim Pitman of FireflyInx.com for layout and design. The cover art I did, and am grateful to Gabriel Horn, Carises Horn and Phyllis A. Fast for allowing me to use their work in the collage. Sgi and blessings to all!

MariJo Moore
In the mountains of western NC
January 2016

THE VISIT

Dean K. Hutchins

It has been a long journey. But now you are resting comfortably here on the last stop of visits to family and dear friends. You saved your granddaughter for last even though she is first in your heart. The week has gone by pleasantly but quickly as you watched her play, and looked over her shoulder as she drew pictures in the book you gave her for her third birthday. You can see that she will grow up into a fine young woman and it fills you with pride.

The house is nearly quiet as the family settles in for the evening. But you are restless and wander into the family room where all the pictures from this and previous generations are proudly displayed. You smile as you once again see the faces of those you have visited in the past few months, as well as those who you expect you will visit with next.

As you head back upstairs, you enter the room where you always stay when you come to visit your son and his family. It's a small room down the hall from the master bedroom and right next to your granddaughter's room. As you open your senses to the world around you, you can faintly hear the unmistakable sounds of lovemaking and you sense that another spirit is entering this world tonight. It makes you smile as you think of your granddaughter. Soon she will have a little brother. But your smile fades as your heightened senses bring another message; whimpering sounds, two of them.

You enter Granddaughter's room to find it filled with thick, acrid smoke. You make your way to her bed where she is frozen in fear under the covers. You talk to her gently in a low voice to try to pacify her, to help her to get out, but you can see that the fire, which started inside the wall, is now leaping across the doorway like a flag flapping in a violent wind. Your voice calms her and you find that you can create an air pocket under the covers so she can breathe.

You hear more whimpering and look under the bed, where the puppy you bought her last year is staring out at the fire. You lean over and softly explain to him what must be done. His ears perk up and he listens intently. Then when you give him the signal, he runs out past the flames, down the hall, and begins barking wildly. Seconds later, your son rushes into the room, grabs your granddaughter out of the bed, and you all leave to wait for the firefighters to arrive.

Thankfully the damage was minimal, but it will be several weeks before her room is livable again. You join the family as they survey the damage.

"You were very brave, and it's a good thing Scout came to wake us up"

"It was OK, Grandpa was here with me, and he's the one who told Scout to go and get you."

"Grandpa couldn't have been here, Baby. You know he's traveling now."

"He was! There was a lot of smoke but I could hear his voice and I recognized his smile!"

She points to a partially burnt picture of you on her wall; the one that used to hang in the family room; the one she insisted she have for her room the day after your funeral. Her parents look at each other and say nothing more.

The next afternoon, after Granddaughter has moved into your old room, you decide it's a good time to leave. You go downstairs where the family is having lunch to say goodbye, but Granddaughter has matured virtually overnight and she can't hear you anymore. Still, that too makes you smile.

Your year is up and it's time to move on to the next plane where other relatives will be waiting. A sense of excitement comes over you and you can't wait to see what comes next. As you walk out through the front door, only the dog says goodbye.

ζ

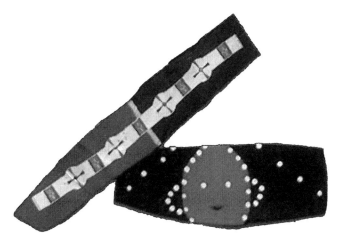

Ten Days in June

Jim Stevens

He had been living in this place for a while. He was up on the bluff in the city called Four Lakes. It was where he felt at home, and his abode was in a neighborhood set right down upon a towering mass of stone. Here one would be led by the crows who circled incessantly, so supremely brash and calling in their own tongues from deep in the trees.

A place such as this, he knew, held the stories of the world. He sensed there was a Grandfather who was speaking his stories from the deep fissures in the rock. The energy here was as if a solar flare had entered the earth from far above, much as with the dropped feather of a hermit thrush, and the light brought into being the shadows beneath the grass and the leaves.

There was a canyon, which cut through these

naked bluffs, and they held their own special secrets. One thing he had heard was that during the nineteenth century, Black Sparrow Hawk had passed through here, leading his people away from the soldiers, toward their homeland on the Wisconsin River further north. In those days, the rock faces on both sides would have watched their passage.

In the days of our story, the grass and forest parks on either side of the canyon were places for him to drift away from the hard streets that covered the neighborhood. On one side, to the north, were Quarry Park and her maze of trails. Once the rock here was dug up and crushed to be carted far away. Before that, and still, the slopes had the feel of Ohio's Fort Ancient. At the edge of the woods was a mound, which encircled the whole place. It was like a sacred tor, which had once been invaded by early twentieth-century technology.

In the brush atop the rocky ledge, he had found a rough peeled log that became his seat under the sun. Here, above the frame houses and the autos hurrying by, he would fill a world of the canyon with visions and the whispered tonality of his flute.

On the other side of the canyon, to the south, there was a cul-de-sac branching away from the street. It opened unto a path wandering through a small prairie, and then it gradually ascended to the heights of Hoyt Park. On top, at the edge of the woods, he had come upon a waist-high truncated pyramid someone had once fashioned out of concrete. It was covered all over with mysterious faces and forms, and it appeared to carry all those things that were hidden; yet emanated out of the brow of the bluff. It was like one of those traditional tables to which medicine people traveled on special, designated, days.

It was on a Thursday he was walking in the prairie, grieving for the people murdered just the night before by a confused boy who did not know how deep the Spirit went. This assassin who had taken nine lives did not experience the flowers of the world.

And now, he was approaching the tall bluff enclosing the low prairie. In the distance, a hawk was circling, very slowly circling. Immediately in front of him was a butterfly of the most beautiful pale green color he had ever seen. The creature was settled upon a tall stalk of the grass, and slowly waving its wings in the gentle breeze. How marvelous a situation this is, he thought.

And then he found the song he was waiting for, there among the grass.

ζ

the man who arises out of the woods
contains two souls
a luna moth holding along a green stalk
suddenly sees it is a star
two wolves appear and begin breathing in
rhythm with the pale wings
after the creation of the world they all begin
by listening to the dark

ζ

Yet the days ensuing felt heavy in his head
and feet. Even with the song that had entered his
life, it was as if he was waiting for the rude dance
to burst up from the earth. In a realm far below
him, Ancient Twins were struggling against the
impinging of evil, playing the great ball game at the
demands of voracious unlit entities that seemed
to have no beginning and no ending. The cries of
clawed beings were wafting up into the sunlight
world above. It caused him hurt.

In his mind's eye, there remained that most
natural of altars. Hawk, the bold winged, flew at
great heights above the air inhabited by lunar
moth. This spirit, fragile and green, was destined
to live in this wake. We are all in need of this
atonement to the earth, he thought.

Look to the earth, is what Hawk said.

There still were the sharp structures of the rock

faces, and he took all of this deep into his heart. He remembered the story told him by his father. It was of the young man, who, in passing through the log, transformed his poor life into the stream of the sky. And as he came to be sitting upon the rock hill, the ancient grandfather opened up by telling him of the great lore inherent in the universe.

On Friday, he thought about finding a trove of the daisy flower he called wabun. He knew exactly where to find these long stalks, with their yellow-sun faces, the rays emanating in white and tipped in pale redness.

A low loft in the breeze hovered over the concrete slabs of Quarry Park. How they spoke to him! *We shall serve with you, two-legged, if you take us with you.*

Then the maze of clearings in the woods of the park was beckoning to him. The paths stretched like the seams within some ancient world. How the air breathed intensely around him as he headed into the afternoon shaded spaces!

The afternoon sun made a dark mosaic across the grass. The man with bronze skin and dark hair was walking up the brow of the hill. Beyond his shoulder, a small strand of cedar appeared to be following him.

He glanced sharply all around him. There was nothing below in the canyon.

The world seemed so familiar to me, he thought.

He walked from the trees at the cliff-side, past

the clearing of the wabun daisies, onto the path
leading back down to the street. The petals looked
so innocent in his hand.

ﻉ

He saved the flowers in an ornate cut-glass
jar of a round table facing the front door
Early old man spirits of the sandstone arbor,
he called them
Protecting the breeze from bad spirits while
they sang of flight
Catching the roar of sentient beings who
shall forever be held close in their thin long
bodies
They are lords of affinity as fire air earth
water, he thought
Coming into being with no second thought
for their destinies where foretold in the
most distancies of multiverse
Where deep primal chattering carries each
day in a solitude of prayer
And the enclosures of the earth give the most
subtle hint of their fragility
They shall live forever in their awareness
And the hawk that moves between each
successive world of perception
And the moth that is reborn between the
whispers and wilderness of sustenance
They are alive on Mother Earth
Each lunar birth crossing through our
familiar bodies of grieving.

This is the way he found his life was going.

On Monday he went out and he found himself in close attention to the cat-like star beings watching from the shadows of the underbrush. He saw himself coming into a fifth world, in his thousands of years of a time of the sun.

He walked up the shaded path to the top of the cliff. There were trails intertwined all throughout the park. He stopped at a stone grotto for a while, letting go the close notes of his flute to spread across the branches of the heights. The walnut out of which it was made caused the sound to come straight deep and clear, and it projected as from a blowgun.

A red squirrel chattered at him for a while, leaf-side, quieted down as he continued playing, then decided he was nobody and scampered away. Soon he turned his body, allowing the tones to waft above the well of earth, spreading out into the closely cropped grass.

He knew where he wanted to go in the park. He packed up his flute and passed along the trail, up the hillside on his way to the overlook where the houses of the city could be seen settled far below. On top, peering over the railing, it was as if looking into a great creature's mouth. There was a low mist coursing across the distant rooms and lawns. Then it was slowly rolling off.

The man was walking across the top of the short-grass hill. Two wolves were walking with him, one on each side. The well-contained island of spruce, seemingly his other companions, was receding from him lower on the hill. In the far distance, the gray ring of hills was shadowed by the islands of clouds.

Hmm. The world is veritably so complex, he thought. There was no telling where he had been. There was no telling how he was seeing things from a different vantage point.

He thought of Hawk, the one of the weeping eye, who flew into the mysterious distances and brought back the most prescient knowing.

He thought of Moth, who carried in its body the green of the aether and rested upon the wabun that was swaying like a shooting star.

He stood for a while, as if hoping for another glimpse into the depths of the city. It was time for him, he knew, to return to the canyon from atop this great sandstone place. As he walked down the path, inadvertently, he thought, he scraped his arm on the rock surface close beside him. He glanced at his arm, where there was now a spot of blood. He looked closely at the stone wall.

ζ

I am the skin the stone scrapes
before the hunting of the star`
he sang.

ζ

He decided this was a song for the day of the spirit hill.

In the rooms where he had been, he was looking for the hawk to come to him. There were so many rooms in the grass of earth, they had all opened one to another, and some of them were right beside and some of them were far afield yet touching him, they were so close. There was the wind no one had seen which flowed through them all. The different spaces to which he had gone were of different worlds.

The moth's prairie was close to the people of prayer. The flower's hill was so close to the ancient people walking with the skies. There are pockets within the universe, he thought, and they are a labyrinth for our sight.

ح

I am the skin the stone scrapes
before the hunting of the star
he was singing.

ح

Two days later, once again he went to the inner prairie across Bluff Street. There were passels of crows, which he heard scuffling right on one side of the canyon, then on the other side. What were they following, he wondered?

It was Thursday, and he felt he was opening into a day of earth. There was a close wind coming across a house, just perceptible beyond the trees. The clouds were rolling very fast across the sky.

He thought he was standing very alone in the grass under the sun, and holding so still for the flow of night.

Between him and the edge of the lake beyond his left shoulder, the grove of evergreen was receding into the prairie. There were people following him, crossing from a lower hill at their rear. Across the prairie, small stands of trees dotted the slopes to the horizon. The two wolf-dogs were walking purposefully with him. The four-legged at his left was now looking straight into the eye of the spirit camera.

It was crossing dusk now. Over the hills far in the distance, a comet, or perhaps it was a hawk, was dipping into the plasma of the horizon.

He didn't know. The prairie was stretching out into the light of yesterday and the earth was a fulcrum upon which his life was balancing itself. He noticed that the leaves in the far small grove of elms were turning pale. Tomorrow, he thought, there would be a hard rain, thunder and lightning. This would be coming soon enough.

PANTHER LAND

Susan Deer Cloud

Sometimes I play the game of "How far back can I remember?" Compared to what most people tell me about their memories, I think I remember further into the past than most. And I feel further back .... back to before I was born a girl in the Catskill Mountains of New York State, back to what Zen Buddhists call "the face I had before I was born." That face lingered in my small child's face for some years, appearing in the rare Kodak snapshots my parents and a few others took of this female phenomenon in the family. For in my mother's family, I was the only girl child in an extended family of boy cousins .... the family I mainly grew up around, the "Indian side of the family," playing with the boys who got to run freer than girls in the early 1950s. At the same time,

I dwelled within a circle of women comprised of my mother, her three sisters, my maternal grandmother and her sisters. No one ever used words like "matriarchy" and "feminism," but those women were like a coven with their fragrant cooking, shared secrets, magical stories, power dreams and ancient singing that made every atom in my small body weep tears at such tragic minor notes wedded to evocative melodies.

At my current wisdom-hair age, the black-and-white images of my little girl countenance rends my heart as much as the women's songs once did. A soulful watchfulness glimmers back at me over my more than six decades that witnessed the twentieth century's second half metamorphose into a twenty first century of intensified violence, collective nervous breakdown, and drugs legal and illegal used to mask human beings' authentic feelings. But the girl in the snapshots was only starting to learn about masks, and the face she had before she was born still flickered through her new human form. How intense she was. Not one photograph shows a smile, not even a hint of one. The word "epigenetics" is another word that no one spoke back then, although the mothers believed the way they conducted their lives when they were pregnant would affect a baby's personality once it was born. Did the face in the puzzle piece snapshots indicate my mother was sad during the nine months leading up to me? Or did the face carry historical trauma and unspeakable loss inside its seeming untouched newness?

"Smile," some of the grownups would urge me. "Say cheese. You look so cute when you smile. You are prettier when you are smiling."

But I chose to remain silently serious and thoughtful for those Kodak cameras rather than bubbly cute and pretty. When I hold those smudged images in my hands I try to recollect when I learned I was "part Indian," that expression mountain people used for my mother's family and other families of mixed Indigenous lineage. No one used "Native American" or any of the other words that eventually came along as if they would somehow serve as a palliative for the genocide preceding us and in myriad ways is still continuing. We never referred to what was done to us as "genocide." What happened to my mother's family was so immense, so buried in a way that would enable us to survive, that we continually dwelled at the event horizon of what wounded many Catskill Indians into near wordlessness.

Perhaps I initially glimpsed the complexity of my being when my mother gave me a brown-skinned doll and said her name was "Pocahontas." She added that the tiny doll with glassy eyes was Indian. "She's like you," my mother lilted. We were in the cellar near the old wringer washer when she placed Pocahontas into my arms and I pulled her close to me among the cobwebs and the spiders. If I tipped Pocahontas far enough her eyes shut

with a click I found to be fascinating. If I tipped
her nearly upside down she emitted a cry like
a cat's meow. I stood in the cellar shadows and
sump pump stench, wishing my mother had given
me a meowing kitten instead of a doll. I hated
it when other girls on the street wanted me to
"play house" with them and our collective dollies,
their pretend domestic life boring me cross-eyed.
Instead, I sought refuge with the boys …. yes, those
unwashed boys who "acted like wild Indians."

But I had been taught to be courteous and
respectful to my elders, so I peered up at my
mother and piped, "Thank you, Mommy." I even
smiled, especially when she hugged me hugging
the gift of Pocahontas.

I didn't know it then, but my mother could not
have given me a more perfect doll. Many years
later when I began seeking out the truth about
Pocahontas, I learned especially through Paula
Gunn Allen's biography of the Powhatan "princess"
that she was a free-spirited, playful, dreamer
girl who had a secret name, Matoaka, "Bright
Stream Between the Hills." I, too, was a girl free-
spirited, mischievous, and given to having vivid
daydreams and powerful night dreams. In my
pre-kindergarten world of spending every waking
wondrous day in woods and meadows, by rivers
and lakes, I did not notice any boundaries between
the so-called "real world" and the world of my
dreaming. All was as fluid as mountain creeks
and high air currents, a weave of land and sky

and spirit realms. I could have been living when Pocahontas lived and the invaders had not yet erected all their harsh barriers for ripping us from that which was our most real world, trying to force us into their terrorizing anti-life of money, rape and ownership.

And, oh, those spirit realms! I was surrounded by women who in the privacy of their homes spoke openly about spirits, visitations, and dreams. When they talked about that aspect of their lives, their eyes shone and their skins and faces emanated light. Even in winter, if I cuddled up next to them it felt as if I were basking in spring sunlight. It seemed as if snow country was about to burst into multiple blossoms. Sometimes I would wake in the deeps of the nights and discern some ethereal form standing at the bedroom door, watching me. At first my heart nearly jumped through my small chest, but soon I grew accustomed to the spirits who reminded me of the picture of a guardian angel my parents hung over my younger brother's and my beds.

Many dreams I had, dreams as vividly populated with people and animals and birds and all manner of wildlife as my waking hours were. After every sunrise we would tell dreams to each other at the breakfast table, still partly asleep, our voices quiet as the country nights. One morning after my father had left for work and my brothers had dashed outside to play, my mother warned, "Susie, make sure you don't tell people outside our family your belief in dreams. If you do, they will think you are crazy and might steal you away and lock you up." I sat across from her in shock. Didn't everybody dream the way we did? Didn't everyone pattern their lives around the deep stories and wise messages of their dreams? Didn't their dreams show them what paths to walk on?

My mother's lips had tightened into two tomahawk blades, though, always a sign that she meant what she said and it would be perilous to ignore her words to me.

"Okay," I whispered. "I won't tell anyone about our dreaming."

There came dreams I did not even tell to her, let alone to my grandmother, aunts and great aunts. Perhaps it was because even as young as three or four I already understood that as much as my future life would always be entwined with their lives, it would also break off from that in their existence which elicited rebellion in me. I didn't want to dwell in a house with a husband and children for all my days. I did not want to be hemmed in by an isolated small town and non-dreamer gossips. I didn't want to spend hours and hours cooking and sewing, ironing and mopping. Already I was a storyteller who knew she was destined to be a writer. When my father took us for rides in the mountains, we would sing songs that we knew, the forests flashing by us in our happiness. But when we could no longer recall more songs, I would make up narratives and sing them while the old Chevy jounced over the dirt roads. Sometimes my family would laugh at me, tease the ebullient little daughter and sister singing stories arising out of seemingly nowhere.

The summer I was four, soon to start kindergarten, I had my first dream of a kind that in later years I came to dub "power dreams." The dream arrived after an evening of watching and catching fireflies, releasing several into jars with punctured lids so my baby brother and I could fall asleep to their flashings. How enthralled we were by the fireflies, some an ethereal green and others a silken gold. Theirs was a Morse code of light, and we pretended they were sending us messages that only we could decipher.

Maybe their messages told the spirits who appeared in my dream to show themselves to me, for somewhere in the deeps of that night I found myself standing in an opening in the woods behind our house, further in than I had ever been taken to. I swayed inside a circle canopied by stars so thick the sky glowed violet white, the grass-and-moss round bejeweled by women I knew to be witches. Around my bare feet shone a scattering of holes, into which the longhaired women easily flew then floated up through other ones. Watching them in their rainbow dresses woven of spider webs, beholding their dream catcher faces flashing centuries of medicine; I recognized that I belonged with them. But I didn't speak my understanding. I didn't have to. They swirled around me, singing poems and stories as I did on long mountain meanders, "Yes, child, you will one day enter into our wildflower ring, fly down into the shining circles and Mother Earth. And you will fly back up; soar sparkling as far as the farthest stars you are made of. But not yet, not yet. You will recognize the day when you are ready to fly like us."

The dawn of the dream I slid slowly out of my twin bed, praying I would not wake up my baby brother who slept parallel to me. I gazed up at the angel who protected us every night so the bogeyman wouldn't invade our bedroom and steal us from our family. The angel had long golden tresses streaming down over a spring green dress flowing down to equally green Earth. She held her open hands out protectively towards a little girl and boy, two innocent children. My father was already up, making his Eight O'clock drip coffee in the kitchen, so I sneaked out the front door and on to the woods behind our house. The woods my mother did not allow me to go into unless she was with me. I had never disobeyed her before that morning, but I wanted to see if I could find where the witches who flew like birds lived.

Gingerly I tiptoed across the wooden bridge my father and grandfather had built, trudged up the railroad tie steps set into a bank, until finally I pirouetted triumphant atop higher land. All the forest and its mysteries stretched out before my red-sneakered feet. And, no camera in sight, I was smiling and smiling. I glanced behind me

.... no mother catching me in my four-year-old rebellion. The morning songbirds serenaded me and very softly I began singing stories that flashed like fireflies through my mind, words in greens and golds, harmonizing with Mother Earth's other two-leggeds. Fearless, protected by the beautiful witches and guardian angel, I skipped down the path other feet had fashioned, sunlight streaming through evergreen branches and between hardwood trunks. Butterflies whirled around me just like the witches in my dream, while the fragrant wildflowers, moss, and pine needles smelled so sweet I felt nearly delirious.

Then the scream. I stopped in the middle of the path, unable to move or speak just as I could not move or cry for help in my nightmares.

"Mommy?" My voice managed to choke out one hopeful word.

But the scream came tearing through the warming air again like an icy current, high pitched, sounding ragged, wounded, angry and terrified. And terrifying. Then I knew. As much as I had recognized the witches in my dream, I realized that I was hearing a Catskill panther in our woods. Was it screaming from that circle in the forest of my dreaming? And why was I hearing it? Didn't people claim the panthers were all extinct, just as there were white people who claimed that all of us Eastern Woodlands Indians were dead? Massacred out of existence forever?

The scream flamed down into my heart, that

voice of the magnificent catamount, that resistance of a kindred spirit making itself known to a curious little dreamer girl. Was I hearing the last Catskill panther on Earth? Was it telling me the panthers were only doing what we "part Indians" were doing, lying low, not showing themselves so they would survive? The scream made my heart pound faster and harder, like the drums of war.

Then it yowled louder. I managed to shake the paralysis out of my bug-bitten legs, turn, and race back towards my family's house. But not before I spotted a great sinewy shape stretched across a high oak limb. Not before the eyes glowed into my eyes in such a way that I would never see anything in the same way again. The panther's eyes took up residence in my very heart, its wildness of seeing in a gold and different light. The great cat's screams sounded like a woman's sobs, as though she had lost everything and everybody she had ever loved.

I raced down the rail tie steps, across the bridge, and up the steps leading to our kitchen door, nearly falling into the room that my father had thankfully left for his long day of work. At that age, I never peered into mirrors, but I had some sense that if my father or anyone else saw me after my encounter with the panther I would exert the same effect on them that the panther had on me. I stumbled into the bathroom and splashed cooling water over my freckled face, neck, arms and legs, shaking as much as I had been frozen before.

When my mother sleepily walked into the kitchen and started making pancakes with wild blueberries for breakfast, I did not share my dream of the witches or the visit of the panther.

That September, I was sent off to kindergarten in the large brick school on the other side of the street. Had I known about symbols then, I might have thought how symbolic for a "part Indian" girl like me to live in a place wedged between a school of "white man" learning and a forest of Indian learning. Every morning I crossed that border of asphalt road to learn how to read, write, think, and become civilized in the manner the teachers defined as "civilized." Every afternoon I crossed back over to the green stucco house, tore off my school dress, shimmied into corduroy pants and flannel shirt, and returned to playing with the boys. Only now there was a difference. Every so often I sneaked back into the woods alone, trying hard not to lose the witches and the Catskill panther who had shown themselves to me.

Not until my early forties, after my mother died of breast cancer and my professor husband yanked my long hair so hard one day I suffered a whiplash injury and nervous breakdown, did I dream again about the circular opening in the night forest. Only this time when I found myself standing there, an educated woman and published writer of many experiences, it wasn't the flying women who appeared to me. Instead, an old Indian man approached me in blue moon light cascading down from Sky World. June fireflies flashed all around him, landing on his head and limbs until they formed a green-gold halo. I wondered if he were some relative from the past, a warrior returned to rescue me from being so beaten down into fear I did not even call the cops after I was hurt into pain so excruciating every molecule in my body screamed like the Catskill panther. Just another Indian woman battered by a white man, no longer trusting that anyone was left on Earth to be tender to her.

"My name is Deer Cloud," the man spoke gently. "I am giving you my name. It will guide you in your visions and writing and all you must do from now on."

And the ancient man with long silver braids gathered my mute brokenness into his arms as if I were the little girl from long ago, began round dancing with me until I felt the way Sky Woman must have felt when she tumbled safely onto Turtle's back and danced until she created Turtle Island. Soon I was flying like the women in their rainbow dresses woven of spider webs. The elder and I flew laughing into the glowing holes then soared back up towards the stars, bare feet shape-shifting into eagle's wings. I, Deer Cloud, was ready to dazzle with the witches. If only I could have told my mother this dream.

NABIITA, A HOUSE SPIRIT

Phyllis Ann Fast

She was there just when I needed strength to unpack yet another box in yet another place to live. Instead I felt a kind and tender otherness on that day. Shorter than me by at least a foot, she didn't seem to notice. I did. I'm only five one. She was short. Nonetheless, I felt her resilience and became resilient myself. She obeyed the spirit of order and thought I did as well. Something about her was Native American. Swinomish? Salish? I'm Athabascan. Very different from her. Besides, she didn't respond to those tribal names. She seemed to be wearing some sort of sleeveless overdress that kept her other clothes clean. It might have been made of animal hide rather than cotton. I couldn't tell. Maybe she couldn't either.

I had just moved to Whidbey Island in

Washington. With sixty-nine not-so-fresh years under my salt-and-pepper hair (emphasis on the salt as there's not much pepper left), I didn't have enough oomph a month after the mover dumped a bunch of boxes in my back bedroom to do much except look. I had felt fairly strong and competent during the first thirty days. Days with my regular spirits. They had other specialties, and putting things away wasn't among them. On the thirty-first morning I stood in the doorway of that spare bedroom and stared with glum eyes.

I felt a hand insert itself into mine and my eyes traveled to a plastic box that I'd loaded with a mishmash of stuff. She led me to the box and took out the stuff she didn't want. I sipped coffee and wondered if I should laugh. She was serious. I didn't laugh. Pretty soon the box held only hangers for pictures, wire for the backings and a few tacks. I felt energy flow through old veins, enough to hang five photos and a painting. I felt almost fifty, well maybe fifty-five. I felt happy. Maybe they're the same thing.

A trip to the store gave me two packets of picture-hanging stuff and more of the tape-on type of hangers. I went through six boxes before the end of the day. That's when she confided her name to me.

Nabiita.

Or it could have been Labiita. She tried to explain what it sounded like: NA-bee-tah. The next time she blew it into my head, it seemed like she told me Labiita. She didn't have a mouth or sound like anything. Not a problem. For one month she made life work.

There were penalties: I had to put my (suddenly hers) hammer, measuring tape and screwdrivers away after every use. They had to go back to the exact same spot I'd stashed them. Her rules. Not mine. When the day's toil wiped me out and I tried to go to bed without putting them in the right places, I'd feel the heavy frown. If I ignored the frown, I'd find myself getting out of my cozy bed within a half hour and—you got it—putting her tools away. She didn't care about dishes or other things that might have been left undone. Just her stuff. Thirty days of youthful energy around me made it worthwhile.

I got fifty-five paintings and other artworks up. "We'd" (Nabiita and I) counted them at least twice a day. On the twenty-ninth day my legs ached so much that I couldn't climb the two-step ladder. She gripped my hand in her immaterial one and stood me beside the little ladder. She wanted me to ascend. My poor legs wanted to rest.

"No, Nabiita," I wailed. "I can't do it today. Let's take a day off."

For someone as bossy as was Nabiita, you'd think I could hear her voice or feel her form words, but I didn't—just her name. I could hear her form her name as if knitting it into my very bones. She used other techniques to convey ideas to me. Nabiita led me to my only calendar and had me fasten my eyes onto the blocked out day that showed me when my cousins would arrive. Then she walked me around the tiny condo and we once again counted all that she and I had accomplished in twenty-nine days. Fifty-five paintings. I'm a painter. They were my artworks. I felt pride. She felt stern.

How does a puff of air feel stern? I'm not sure, but Nabiita managed it. She made it obvious that she wouldn't tolerate my laziness and that she owned the work we had done.

Somehow I realized her quota consisted of sixty paintings. Five to go. Ugh. She wanted them on the wall by this, the thirtieth day. Okay. I forced wobbly legs to go up onto the ladder to make her kind of measurements. My style was to wing it. If I had been left to do it alone I would have nailed a bunch up without counting and without regard to inches or to where the hanging wire stretched. Artists don't care about those things!

Nabiita cared. We measured from the bottom to where the nail would be once the painting had been there for a day or so. When we got one done, I'd find myself climbing off the ladder, backing up a few feet and eyeing how well I had done.

Never well enough. Out of the eventual sixty paintings that now hang on my walls, at least fifty of them had to be re-positioned. Thanks to her relentlessness, it feels like home, my home. I was proud to show off my artworks to my cousins on that thirty-first day. It looked like I had lived there for years.

We spent a happy couple of days together, my cousins and I. As usual, all of the spirits seem to melt away when I've got company. That's why I didn't miss her. I didn't sense that Nabiita was missing from me or my new home until after I bid adieu to my cousins. I felt the safety of the four spirit guides who have been with me for all my life, painting with me, writing with me, teaching with me, and occasionally doing housework with me. In the coming days I expected to keep on working with Nabiita to put away the rest of my things. My spirit guides prepared me to face the truth: Nabiita was a project spirit, one who came to me for one purpose: sixty paintings.

I miss her and wish she would come back. Goodbye, Nabiita, and thank you for all your help.

ζ

Almost Ten Months Before You Were Born

MariJo Moore

Five elderly women sat circling an eclipsing fire, shawls covering their heads as if they were hiding from the shadows. One whistled. One threw grass and dead flowers in the blue flames. Two sucked on sassafras root sticks, pretending their throats were sore, and one cried non-existent tears.

"She's really gone. Back to the same area. I know she has," one of the two sucking on sassafras sticks said without removing the stick from her mouth. The listening fire crackled in agreement, but not one of the women acknowledged her.

The night grew darker and the fire spoke louder. The five continued to ignore her; as if her flaming tongues were spectacles for which they had no eyes, as if her hot white ashes were redundant playthings to be buried later. The fire gobbled at the wood and spat sparks at the wizened women. One spark landed on the hem of the whistling woman's shawl. She sucked in her breath for a moment, slapped out the spark, brushed away the singed remnants, and then continued to whistle. None of the others commented on the happening.

"I wish she hadn't left. I still had some concerns to go over with her. Still had some concerns to go over with her." The woman who was feeding the fire repeated herself. "Still had some concerns to go over with her. She said she was ready to go back, but I didn't believe her. So much going on in the Indian world today. So much that is misinterpreted by so many."

"I did," hissed the spirit of the fire. "I knew she was ready to go back when she told me so over a month ago. She wants to help make changes."

The women continued to ignore the fire's curling, smoking words.

"Well," said the one with a hole burned in her shawl," she is gone now so there isn't anything we can do about the prospects we wanted to go over with her as a spirit. Now, is there?'

"Perhaps," two women said at the same time as they removed sassafras root sticks from their cheeks, but only one continued the sentence, "we should have paid more attention to her and what she was sharing from her last time there, and then we could have gone back with her."

"I wouldn't have gone with her! No way would I have gone where she had chosen to be born this time, wanting to go back into that same confused existence!" The woman crying non-existent tears yelled in a menacing, scratchy voice. "And neither would any of you!" she added as she raised her hand and made a semi-circle, pointing toward each of the others.

"I would have gone with her had she asked," the fire spoke more weakly now. She was tired of eating grass and dead flowers and her stomach was fanning out. "I would have gone anywhere with her, kept her warm while she attempted the changes she wanted to make. She fed me oak baskets and hemlock loaves, and never left me untended as you five often do."

The whistling woman stopped whistling. A sour breath of wind came out of seemingly nowhere, bringing a hiccough from the woman with a lap full of grass and dead flowers. She stood up, the contents of her skirt fell to the ground as the fire watched in horror as she felt the woman's desire to stomp her out. The woman didn't; she sat back down. The fire relaxed.

Quietness came upon the circle of five. Cold quietness like the squishing of wet moss, stepped on intentionally. The fire tried to pop through the quietness, but she was too feeble and her blistered tongues were tired. It was time for darkness to cover all.

The fire died, its spirit creeping into the realm

nearby.

The women sat and stared at the empty fire hole. In silence they sat in the widening night, ignoring one another's loudening thoughts of where each would have to go in her next full materialization. Knowing in their hearts that for now, they would have to be unfailing in visiting and helping the one who had chosen to go back.

HOUSE OF PORTALS

Lois Red Elk

ζ

The house of portals takes my story from once upon a time to this present room where a resurrected eagle and hawk have winged their way to my personal space. Their essence perches in the living room context and listens for something moving, as dreams take a quantum leap into my sunrise.

ζ

The Grandpas were out hunting one day and decided to move toward the river, hoping to surprise deer drinking from the backwaters of the Missouri River. They had been out on the flat

land all day and hadn't seen any game. They drove
down the gravel road and headed south past
Parkers old abandoned log house then turned east.
As they drove under the high wires that crossed
over the woods, Grandpa Eddie saw a dark shadow
in the ditch that looked like some dog had been
hit. He slowed and as they got closer they noticed
a large wing laid out across the spear grass.
Grandpa knew immediately what it was and what
happened. Many times eagles and hawks sit up on
the tall electrical poles and once in a while one of
them would be shocked to death when their claws
create a short circuit.

That is what happened. The large eagle lay
silent below the power pole, its wing fanned out
like it was ready to bless a ceremony or ready to
lead a headman dancer into the dance arena. Both
the Grandpas jumped out of the truck and slowly
made their way down the ditch toward the eagle's
body. They always carried sage and tobacco in
their pockets, never knowing when a thank you
offering would be made to the earth or the sky.

Grandpa Eddie looked at the beautiful winged
one, the one who so dutifully carries prayers and
protects the sacred walk of holy ones. He knew
what to do. As he and his cousin spoke in Dakota,
he opened his pouch of tobacco; they bowed
their heads and proceeded to acknowledge the
spirit that was surrendered at that place. One of
the Grandpas sang a short song and offered the
tobacco. They stood and observed the magnificent

bird and remembered all the stories they had heard about the flying relatives. Grandpa took off his jacket and gently wrapped the eagle, covering the head and folding the wings. I remember one of my Grandmas telling how large the eagles can grow. This one was three feet tall and weighed several pounds.

When they brought the eagle home, more prayers were said. They had to wait for a few days before they took the feathers and removed the head. After several family members came to the house to look at the eagle, It was decided that one of the grandsons needed a staff and this eagle would go to that young grandson. Later the young man went to Korea and when he returned he shared with the elders all his dreams and how the eagle spoke with him and guided his walk all through that foreign land. His family passed the staff on down to the descendants and to this day the family carries it respectfully.

ζ

This yard, this house, this open heart accepts their prayers and welcomes the carved cottonwood bowl to my hair for cleansing with sage smoke. It is then I know we are all one for this early morning nourishment of earth presence where no famine lingers, only the domain of harmonious spirits.

ζ

In our Ospaye (family) all the members dance the traditional style. Grandma says it is one of the best ways to keep the culture alive. Every time I went to visit Grandma she was beading or making a dance outfit for one of the family. She kept all her beads sorted by color, stored in old mason jars and stacked on a little bookshelf next to her worktable. Her worktable. It was a maze of wood, deer hide, beads and stones. I would sit at the table and look at the pieces of tanned hide in a shoebox. Some were about 6 x 6 inches, others were twice that size, neatly folded, and other pieces still had the fur of the animal on the edges. I asked her what she was going to make from all the pieces and she would always tell me the designs hadn't come to her yet. One piece she was beading was going to be a rosette. She had already made 4 of them, each a little larger than the other. I always wanted to touch the dyed quills, they were so shiny and colorful, but I learned a lesson about barbs so left them alone. On the side of the table next to a wooden loom she had a small wooden bowl made from the knot of a tree. Inside the bowl I noticed the residue of burned grass. I wanted to ask her what she was burning but my mother told me to stop asking so many questions. I do remember the slight aroma of sweet grass in her hair when she lifted me into her arms, hugged me and whispered to me in Dakota.

ζ

I walk in moccasins made of sacrificed deer hide, not for running or escaping but walking purposefully down the hallway that daily transforms from a rug to a path of fresh grass where I recognize an echo off limber air next to Grandma's vibrating neutrinos. They have assembled and greet me at my bedroom door.

ζ

I learned how to bead watching my Grandmas and my mother. As a child I would sit hours at a time observing them select colors, draw designs, cut shapes, pull sinew apart into threads an then start with 5 beads at a time on one edge of the deer skin. Weeks later I was always amazed at how fast and even all the rows of beads lay flat over the entire moccasin. One day Grandma gave me a piece of deerskin and a threaded needle. There was no question in my mind about what to do, where to start. I was excited to be sitting with Grandma, doing was she did so proficiently. Of course I would do well; sitting next to her was like sitting next to the one who could do everything. She hummed, she was steady, she was patient, she accomplished so many projects, she guided me through a world of creation and she prayed always. I watched as she would glace at the staff hanging off the wall, her lips moved as if she was talking to someone she knew well, as if she was listening and then responding.

ζ

We unite as our energy embraces a common cloak, a common mind of belief and love, and instantly I am standing next to her at the wooden table in the log house Grandpa built, where she sews quilt pieces made into blankets that yawn prayers over all lives she protects. My life, too, shielded in the stitches and blood.

ζ

When I was in my teens, my aunt shared with me an amazing story that I will always cherish as part of my being as a Lakota. I had been having many dreams about relatives that seemed like riddles that needed to be solved. I shared the dilemma with my father who took me to my aunt. What she revealed to me was the knowledge that our family belonged to a dream society and that my Grandma was known as a dream interpreter. Dreams were an important and integral part of the Lakota life. I remember as a child the excitement and celebration that followed after we children shared a dream. It was taken for granted that this was the routine. It was in my teens that the dreams became more complex. Again, Grandma's knowledge was reaching me, and my aunts and parents were the conduit for translating what it all meant. The D/Lakota culture embraces many kinds of societies. The purpose of these societies is to aid individuals, and warrior and women's groups with spiritual support. This belief honors the spirits and prepares us for any questions or difficulties we may have in this earth life. The societies also aid us to accept, face and welcome the unknown.

ζ

I close my eyes as she brings forward her presence where we sense and listen to thoughts as they synchronize from similar genes. We speak in her dialect, the words I dreamed last night, then feel the beginnings that keep us connected, make us whole for this road of uneven forces and odd events.

ζ

The Dream Culture of the Lakota is complex. I don't claim to understand the entire culture. I do know that there is another part of our lives that our people identify as 'our other selves' and that we have to take care of that life just like we care for our daily awake life because it is sacred. The D/Lakota language is unique in that it contains words that explain the sacred world or dream world. Sometimes I dream in Lakota and hear words that are unfamiliar. I am told that only a spiritual leader can interpret the words. When the Grandparents spoke in D/Lakota, or when they prayed, they sometimes moved into a different language briefly then moved back to the common language again. They did that to acknowledge among themselves and the spirits that they were in a sacred realm and trusted that their language and prayers would keep them focused.

ζ

We speak this way, mind to mind, and have done so all my life as planned from the other world. Now it is the moment, time to burn cedar for her precious words and burn sweet grass for he grace as I accept this oath, this unbreakable love between all space and all that moves. We bring presence where our portals open.

ζ

During WWII, my parents moved to Seattle to look for work. They were both talented ingenious people who could easily participate in any setting. They were both survivors. Father was an arc welder and found work quickly in the shipyards. Mom, seeing how easily Dad found work and how well he was paid asked Dad to teach her to weld. The family moved back and forth between the West coast and the reservation. One year my father was notified that he was needed back home, his aunt had passed away. She was like a mother to him and it was difficult to not be a part of the last days of his elders. We children did not know the Grandmas were passing away. We didn't understand the concept of human death. When we arrived back to the reservation the first person I wanted to see was my favorite Grandma. I was told that she went visiting down the river and over the bridge to see her other relatives. I immediately wanted to go.

I had at one time been taken for a ride on an old ferry near the Poplar River and in my mind that would be an exciting trip. I was told that it would take a long time and that we had to go back to Seattle. I kept asking about her, when was she coming home, would it be tomorrow? I was assured that I would see again later and that she just might come and visit us in Seattle. For many months I wondered how she was, what she was doing and was always assured that she was fine. In my young mind I set the matter aside. Eventually public school, reservation life and prejudice over took all my attention. I lost track of time. Eventually I learned of death and funerals, but never thought that death had taken my Grandmas.

One night I dreamed of my Grandma. She was with several other elderly ladies. I described the dream to my dad and he told me those were my relatives and that my Grandma came to visit me in my dream and that was the way all the relatives would visit. And it has been that way since. I experienced and became aware of how important the dream world is to us. I still have the little moccasins she made for me, the quilled hair ties she made and placed on my braids, the little kettle she used to carry her soup in. And our family has the eagle staff that has guided the relatives through the years. These handmade pieces are connections that stand for history, culture, spirit and most of all guide us to our portals and bring us closer to the ancestors. Always when I dream of the Grandmas I light sweet grass. It pleases them.

MOTHERLESS

GABRIEL HORN

REVELATIONS OF A STORY

Gabriel Horn (White Deer of Autumn)

I blinked, scanning my surroundings, and becoming fully conscious, I walked. The tall spirit alongside of me was walking too, no, more like gliding, guiding me up a thin groove of trail on what I somehow understood upon reflection, was the back of an ancient turtle mound. Shafts of sunlight penetrated a light mist, the kind you see in early morning, while the air itself emanated a sweet and earthy scent. Spiraling always higher, we moved through an overgrowth of lush and luminescent shades of green. In time, we had reached the top. And there, where we paused, the spirit gestured, and my eyes followed, peering through a small opening overlooking an immense expanse of Ocean. In all my life, I had never seen such beauty, and over the course of sixty-five years, I had seen beauty.... The spirit of beauty sustained my existence. I had often as a child, and an older man, wounded and in need of something beautiful, watched the sun setting into the sea, the liquid fire flaring upward to the evening sky, the radiant colors painted across the horizon as a myriad of water birds would wing on their sky trails toward their sanctuaries, a dolphin breaching just beyond the breaking waves, the dorsal shimmering. Indeed, I had seen the spirit of beauty, and it healed me.... I saw it often in the faces of my children when they were happy, and in sadder moments, I saw the spirit in their grieving tears as well. I had seen it in so many faces of children I can't count them all. I saw it in the women and men who had loved me, and the ones who loved me now. As a little boy schooled among the nuns and priests, I would catch sight of that spirit beyond their empty eyes, seeing it in trees and grasses; in clouds and sky; and in sometimes birds or animals that happened by....

When I was a young teacher in 1974, shadow men with badges invaded our Heart of the Earth school, pointing guns at my head, and yet such as they were, these men could not prevent the beauty there was in the spirit of the Indian children standing in defense behind me.

Even living in the housing projects of Minneapolis, I would seek out the beauty. With my black lab E in the passenger seat, and the sacred Pipe in the back, we would ride in my '69 Mustang at first light, to a secret place, park on a vacant street, and together we slipped and slid our way down icy embankments and a dangerous ridge to reach the cold shore of the Mississippi, where we would sit sometimes on a patch of hard sand in the snow at the river's edge, and we would see the beauty, and with the Pipe in my hands, the young teacher I was then would smoke my prayers to the Mystery, for the Spirit of Beauty in All Things to hear....

But, at this moment, in this place and time, a spirit stands with me sharing this sacred place on an ancient turtle mound, where the beauty of Ocean seems endless....

I understood then, that in the most profound part of my consciousness, I would never forget the sight of the blue/green turquoise water scintillating, and beckoning, in that brief moment before out of what I imagine was pure instinct, I had made that sudden turn.

Behind me, three turtles, two young ones and a mother, dropped down into a shallow crevice concealed by the jungle and into the currents of a clear and swirling stream. Without warning, a terrible feeling had erupted within me, and an involuntary reaction immediately followed. All at once, I broke away from this sacred place, to follow them, and there I was running barefoot on age-worn knees, tripping and free fall flying over branches and bushes and plants, racing with an urgency of life and death to keep up with the steep declining flow of the three swimming turtles, and why, I did not know....

Approaching the base of the great mound, I veered abruptly away from the stream, plunging and pushing myself through the last of the dense growth, to arrive first where the pure moving water poured out. Still in a race against time, I struck what seemed out of nowhere an invisible force as powerful as a magic shield, and it stopped me cold at the edge of hell on Earth. I staggered backwards, and, falling to my knees, I caught sight of the water falling too, and my helpless hands reached out. "No! No! No!" I cried, but the turtles, one by one by one, carried in the liquid life-force of their new beginnings fell themselves into a clustered capture of plastic bags and bottles and broken objects of all kinds, and silicone and boron and gallium and phosphorus and arsenic, and oil slicks and chemical spills and sewage runoff from city streets and cruise ships and tankers and coal plants and factories and mines, and suburban lawns, and the rusted hooks and lures of the sportsmen's fishing lines, and the dead and dying fish and crabs, the decayed cetacean, each entangled in discarded nets of the fishing industry and its ten thousand vessels, and Styrofoam pieces of coolers and cups and buoys and busted boogie boards and deflated birthday balloons, and cigarette butts, from the tourists and partygoers and vacationers. Everything wrong with the civilized world, coagulated, floating on and below the surface of what once, I deduced, had been a tide pool now turned cesspool.

Horror-struck, I could only watch as the Mother and two young turtles trapped in the human debris, struggled for their lives. And yet, there! a slight shift, and a wave moving the surface of the sludge, and a trace of hope returned, when there was no hope left at all; for the timing of the turtles' descent so synchronized with the rising and ebbing tides, I could see they felt the tugging of the Ocean, wanting them, needing them, loving them into the deeper part of herself as she has been doing for 200 million years. A firm and gentle touch of both strength and love had grasped my shoulder, and the spirit looked down, and myself nearly broken, collapsed on the littered shore, looked up.

At first, I was unaware of the transition the spirit's gaze had caused, nor the synthesis that had occurred. Opening my eyes into yet another state of conscious, I stared at the ceiling in the darkness of my bedroom, weeping, and as I lay alongside my life-companion Amy, I could feel her hand clasping my arm, whispering in half-sleep, "Are you alright, Gabe?"

"Yes," I managed. "Yes, I will be…." In an all-encompassing emotion of immense sorrow for what people have done to the world, I willed myself to sit at the edge of the bed. Trembling, with tears still streaming down my face, I could not yet know in conscious reality, what my unconscious already did; that the spirit of a story had been seeded in my brain.

I understand, that *when the spirits visit*, they can take you places you have no idea of where you're going, nor what you will find or discover. Some are benevolent; some not. I was fortunate, for I was taken to an altered reality in this Great Mystery of limitless possibilities, and in this transformed state of mind, I experienced the conception of creativity that one day would birth a story, and all along in the years of gestation and form that is the storytelling process, I would journey back and forth in both the conscious and unconscious as I wrote, and rewrote, and revised, this novel I would one day call, <u>Motherless</u>.

I was for most of my life, a teacher and professor of literature, and have read many stories; I swear there were days in class when the door would open with a squeak, and they would enter: the spirit of the author, or the spirit of the story itself, or a spirit just wanting to listen. I taught writing too, heard many stories. When I worked in the Indian schools in my youth, I can so clearly remember the orators and poets who stopped by and read to us. The spirit of their orations and the spirit of their poems left words in our minds, playing like music, the strings of our Native hearts. And how intense and proud we would feel when the AIM leaders would steal away from the feds, and stop by for "a talk," some never returning, except in spirit during ceremonies for the imprisoned and the dead. I can close my eyes and recall, even now, forty years later, the elders who visited us as well, storytellers of the old tradition, telling sacred stories, some handed down through generations, and other more personal ones along their life journeys.

Indeed, everything has spirit.

When Amy had read my final draft of _Motherless_, she blessed the bamboo paper pages with her tears, and made me realize, it was a sacred story I was telling too. The spirit in her tears fed the spirit in both the story and me.

Epilog:
The Final Revelation from
the Teller of This Story

The night I determined that I had concluded the story of _Motherless_, I fell asleep, and as I awoke in that altered reality when dreaming and consciousness become one, I found myself alone and barefoot and walking along a beach of bone white sand, and warm water deep blue and luminous in the Full Moon's Mother of Pearl light.

I happened upon a jetty that extended into a small lagoon, and compelled to walk the slippery rocks, I made my way further out. When I paused and gazed down into the water, I spotted a Mother Turtle and two young ones swimming with her. A woman I do not know for certain who, was waving her arms at me from the shore. "Be careful," she called out. I stood acknowledging her concern for an instant, but descending the rocks of the jetty, I refused to concede any fear whatsoever, and stepped into the crystal clear water to be with the turtles.

I stood in the shallows while they encircled me, and reaching with my hands as if invited to do so, I lovingly stroked each of them. Have you ever stood in the water under a full moon and touched a free and living turtle's shell?

Next thing, I am standing on the rocky platform of the jetty once again, but the Mother Turtle had now become a woman and taken her place alongside of me and slightly in front of me. She stood on the lower larger stones where the water lapped. I could only see her from the back; her hair cropped about shoulder length was thick and dark with threads of red streaks, and the exposed skin of her shoulders was a silky copper brown and glistening. I am not consciously aware that I ever saw her face, and though I may have, she was too sacred for me to remember at this time.

But what she did, and that which I will embrace as memory until my dying breath, was hold out her opened hand behind her as she began to step back down into the water, sliding it like a flipper delicately over my own outstretched hand, and without looking up at me, this is what she said....

Thank you... for all you have done.

Then she descended fully into the sea where she transformed once more into the turtle. I watched the three of them as they paddled and swam towards a gate a short distance from where the jetty ended. Having reached it, they paused, and that is where she turned to me, smiling in the way a Turtle Mother smiles. But my enchanted and humbled state became one of sudden apprehension, as she opened the gate, and never turning back again, they left, heading out into the depths and vastness of Ocean and the Unknown....

At daybreak, I sat at my desk in the coral colored room we call our office, putting these final words on the page. My gaze falls then on a ceramic turtle that could fit in your hand, under my computer screen. A child of a dear friend had shaped the turtle in a sixth grade art class, and she gave it to me as a reminder that everything has spirit, everything we create. So don't forget the spirit of the story, Uncle Gabe.As I touched the turtle lightly with my forefinger, the spirit it holds within its glazed green beauty, spoke to me, speaks to me now, telling me, after years of writing and rewriting, It is done. And the journey of a story and the turtle that carries it, has begun....

ζ

Coosewoon's Blue Vision

Clifford E. Trafzer

In 1978, Kenneth Coosewoon participated in the camp gathering composed of directors of Native American drug and alcohol treatment centers in Oklahoma. They met at Dwight Mission. This experience led to Kenneth's Great Vision, one of the most life-changing events in his life. Wallace and Gracie Black Elk led the Swear lodge at the camp in the Cookson Hills near Tahlequah, Oklahoma. The Black Elks had recognized early in their relationship with the Coosewoons that one day Kenneth would be a healer and leader of the Swear lodge and had given him their Chanupa Song way before his great vision.

Kenneth had helped Wallace and Gracie build the swear lodge in a little clearing near Sallisaw Creek. They situated the sacred lodge at the edge of the woods, just downhill from the school's cemetery. They built a fire and began heating the rocks they would use in ceremony. After a few hours, the rocks glowed red hot and Wallace took them into the lodge. They began the religious ceremony with song and prayer. During the ceremony Kenneth "experienced everything" he "didn't know existed," including "moving spirits" and "sparks that jumped around in the darkness of the sweat lodge." He thought someone in the Swear lodge was striking a cigarette lighter, striking the flint down with his thumb and creating sparks in the total darkness inside the lodge. Kenneth recalled, "The sparks started dancing all around me."

Soon after he saw the sparks, or moving spirits through the darkness, he witnessed an old rawhide rattle dancing around him. At first, he thought one of the other participants was shaking the rattle filled with small rocks or seeds, but he soon realized that no one was holding the rattle; it was suspended in the black space in front of him. The rattle acted on its own, moving about Kenneth's body, shaking uncontrollably. He thought the sound of the rattle "was the most beautiful thing I had ever heard." He knew the rattle had spiritual meaning, which seemed to act in concert with the moving spirits or sparks. Today, he believes that the Grandfather or Great Spirit was using the moving sparks and the rattle to cleanse his mind and body, preparing him for a greater prayer and vision. In addition to experiencing moving spirits and a shaking rattle, Kenneth witnessed other spiritual events that became a prelude to his Great Vision.

During the course of the ceremony, Kenneth fixed his eyes on the red glowing rocks in the middle of the lodge. Something in the center of the rocks caught his attention. At first he saw an unusual spark or beam of light. "I looked down at the rocks," he pointed out, and he "could see a little spark down in the rocks." Kenneth kept looking at the spark, which created an intense beam of light "just like a flashlight pen." The long narrow light beamed out of the rocks aimed at Kenneth's heart; he felt the light penetrate his heart and soon he saw blood spurting out of his chest. Although blood squirted out of his heart each time his heart beat, he felt no pain and wondered if this was symbolic of the spirit world "flushing out my meanness." He thought that the Spirit was cleaning his blood, pushing out the evil, meanness, and negative energy.

Kenneth sat in the lodge thinking everyone saw the moving spirits, shaking rattle, piercing light, and blood spurting from his heart. Later he learned this was not the case. Only Kenneth saw the steam of light beaming out of the rocks and onto his heart until the man sitting next to him reported, "Yeah, it's shining right on your heart." Then an eagle appeared in the sweat lodge, blessing Kenneth with each movement of its wings. Kenneth's visions made him feel like he was floating. Although somewhat confused by the spiritual messages, he felt wonderful. In symbolic ways, he was receiving profound spiritual messages that led him to walk "the Good Red Road."

Kenneth compared his experience in Black Elk's sweat lodge ceremony with that of Christians who say they can be reborn into their religion by attending a revival meeting. His spiritual experiences humbled him and taught him a new way. Inside a sacred lodge built on the Mother Earth in the woods of the Cookson Hills, a Comanche took a giant step in his transformation into a world of healing and caring for others.

The Great Vision

At dusk during the course of the sweat lodge ceremony, Kenneth volunteered to take care of the fire outside the lodge. While the rest of the men walked up to the mission to have supper, he kept close watch over the fire, which was heating the rocks to continue the ceremony. Kenneth remained at the campsite and watched the fire to keep it from spreading into the nearby woods and prairie. After everyone had left the site, Kenneth watched the fire explode, sending flaming blue embers into the air and ground. One of the glowing blue embers caught his eye, and he heard a clear voice telling him to pick it up. This was the beginning of a remarkable spiritual visitation or Great Vision where Kenneth received the Blue Medicine that he would use in his healing ceremonies.

When Kenneth heard the voice instruct him to pick up the blue ember, he walked to the glowing charcoal and picked it up. "I kept looking at it and the glowing ember kept getting brighter and brighter. When I first picked it up, it felt a little bit hot and I started to throw it back down." However, the blue ember cooled to his touch, but kept glowing a deep blue in color. It glowed brighter and brighter, bringing forth a deeper vision. Just then, Kenneth said "a big bird " told him to walk down to the creek. At the time, Kenneth did not understand what was taking place but knew it was spiritual. All the time, he held onto the blue ember. "So I had that glowing wooden chip in my hand and as I walked down to where that bird was calling me, that ember started getting brighter and brighter."

Kenneth began to pray while he stood on the creek bank, when all of a sudden, a strong wind blew through the woods and the wind "went right through me and by me." Kenneth looked up into the sky and saw lightning. He heard the roar of thunder. It began to rain slightly, although when he looked up, he saw no clouds and believed it was raining just in that small spot where he stood. He felt as if he was in the middle of the universe, with one sky above and the earth below. He peered out in the various directions and finally saw flashing and zigzag lightning. The entire scene was just "like a movie" and Kenneth was in the middle of a real life drama. By this time, he admitted he was "getting scared" but he simply did not understand the meaning of these dramatic events.

Kenneth began asking himself, "What is all this about?" Then the drama continued when a huge oak "started dancing and shaking." In fact, Kenneth felt "an earthquake all around him as the whole earth shook." The earth shook and trees danced, bouncing him "about ten feet in the air." All of a sudden, he saw two lights coming through the woods beyond the creek and thought people with flashlights might be walking through the forest. The lights had a life of their own and appeared in the black night "like two eyes that blinked." The lights swirled into a ball of blue light, glowing and rolling in the darkness. The ball of light diffused into a florescent fog, moving across Sallisaw Creek. The light circled around Kenneth's body and glowed blue. Kenneth recalled, "I tried to reach down and get some of it and touched it to find out what it was." As he tried to feel the blue foggy light, a voice called out to him, saying, "No, don't touch me!" So Kenneth raised his hand away from the glowing blue light, all the while holding the blue ember in his other hand.

Immediately after withdrawing his hand, the blue light surrounding his body spoke to Kenneth, saying, "I want you to run sweat lodges for me." The spiritual voice was male and spoke to Kenneth as if coming from the blue foggy light. "You run the sweats, " the Spirit said, "and I'll show you how to run them. I will teach you everything you need to know and I'll always be with you. I'll never leave you." The Spirit promised, "You will see many miracles and many good things will happen." The Spirit urged Kenneth to trust in him and promised always to help him with the Swear lodges," provided he would help others.

Kenneth spoke out loud, saying, "I'm no leader of the sweat lodge" and "I don't have anything to run the sweats with." The Spirit answered, saying, "Get a water bucket and a dipper." Kenneth understood the meaning of these instructions since the leader of the sweat lodge used a bucket and dipper to pour water onto the glowing hot rocks inside the sweat lodge. According to Kenneth, the Spirit then said, "Start with that," meaning the water bucket and dipper.

Just as quickly as these events began to occur, they ended. The woods turned silent, except for the sound of the crackling fire. Kenneth looked into his hand to see if the blue ember was still there. He found it still warm within his hand and he saw the chip of wood still appearing blue. He put the chip into his pocket and returned to the fire to add more wood while he contemplated the events that had recently swirled around him. He wondered about the meaning of the messages given to him but he had no interest in leading a sweat lodge ceremony or healing others. That was not what he was about.

When the men returned from Dwight Mission, they continued the sweat lodge ceremony they had started earlier. Kenneth said nothing to the men about what he had experienced. In fact, it was some time before he told anyone about the Great Vision or the Blue Medicine that he had seen glow blue, the chip he had held in his hand. Little did he know it at the time, but the Blue Medicine he held in his hand would be a gift from the Grandfather, a portion of his medicine that he would give to patients to ingest orally into their body as part of the healing process. Throughout his Great Vision, Kenneth had held the Blue Medicine in his hand. At the time he received these medicine gifts, he had no idea of the power given him. He would learn this through personal experience in due time.

Shortly after returning to Medicine Park and Meres, Oklahoma, Kenneth received a call from his daughter asking him to come to the hospital to be with her. Not many hours before, her boyfriend was shot point blank in the liver with a 38-caliber handgun. Reluctantly, Kenneth agreed to meet his daughter at the Lawton Hospital. While preparing to drive into town, he heard the voice he had heard at Dwight Mission. "Kenneth, you do not know the power I have given you. Go and heal James!" When Kenneth reached the hospital, a priest was giving James his last rites, but Kenneth heard the voice saying, "You will do a sweat lodge for him and he will live." Once the priest left, Kenneth whispered as much to James who woke up and blinked his eyes in agreement. Kenneth called his clients from the rehabilitation center who had met him on Cache Creek where they had built a sweat lodge. When everyone entered the lodge, Kenneth admitted that he did not know exactly what to do but he believed that their combined prayer was stronger than his single prayer. So they prayed for James, who stabilized, doctors telling Kenneth that if they could get his blood vessels to flow through the remainder of his liver parts, then James might be flown to Oklahoma City for advanced treatment. Kenneth gave James a small piece of his Blue Medicine, which James ate, taking the healing power into his body.

Meanwhile, Kenneth reassembled his colleagues, and they prayed again. When they came out of the sweat lodge, the opposite creek bank glowed a fluorescent blue glow, which Kenneth considered a "good sign." The blood vessels feeding the liver of James began to flow. He grew sufficiently better so they airlifted him to the University of Oklahoma Medical Center where he slowly recovered. He is alive today, a testimony to Kenneth's gift.

Today, Kenneth believes that the voice is that of Grandfather, the Supreme Being of the universe. Over time, all things he needed came to Kenneth: eagle feathers, tobacco, sage, drum, eagle bone whistle, buffalo skull, prayer stick, and sacred pipe. He uses these gifts in his healing ceremonies to help others. Kenneth is the first to say, "I do not bring the healing and I do not decide who will be healed. Grandfather does the healing and uses me to help others. That was what I am suppose to do, and I have spent most of my life following the instructions given to be in the Great Vision using Blue Medicine."

In 2016, Kenneth Coosewoon continues the work he was asked to do during his spiritual visitation on Sallisaw Creek. He will never quit the work before him; no matter the personal setbacks he has suffered with the loss of his loved ones. Kenneth prays daily, asking for healings for everyone who asks him to use his medicine gifts to benefit others.

Widows and Orphans

Pastor Brother Sequoyah Seeking
Dawn Karima
(For my Godparents)

Pastor Brother Sequoyah sits upright in the feather bed. His wife, Vera Lo, snores, a light rattle hidden in the bridge of her nose. Throughout the fifty-five years of their marriage, Vera Lo has learned to sleep through his fitful nights. This was not always so.

At first, when Pastor Brother Sequoyah would pace their ramshackle house, praying from somewhere deep in his belly, Vera Lo would bury her head under feather pillows and dove-in-the-window quilts. Deep sleep found her that way once, tangled and covered, and pushed a feather into her open mouth. She inhaled, nearly choked on feathery spines and cotton. Since then, she sleeps above the covers and breathes through her nostrils. Pastor Brother Sequoyah's night rambling seems not to trouble her at all.

Pastor Brother Sequoyah wanders out the back door. He paces over the sparse grass and gravel. His bare feet sense nothing under leathery soles and diabetes.

Pastor Brother Sequoyah is a preacher. This is like saying that the Qualla Boundary is a reservation; it is such a matter of local fact. He is sixteen years old, digging ginseng on the other side of the holler along the Oconaluftee River, when a lithe and luminous figure, all lit up from within, simply says, " 'Siyo."

"Say on, Sir," answers Pastor Brother Sequoyah, as calm as if he converses with spirits on an annual, even daily basis. He is a good boy, prone to believing in sgili or haints, but other than that, sensible. The Spirit says simply that Pastor Brother Sequoyah needs to tell people that Edoda, commonly called God, is for them and not against them. Not one to contradict, Pastor Brother Sequoyah nods amiably and sets out to inform The Spirit about a certain point.

Pastor Brother Sequoyah cannot read. The alphabet, road signs, billboards, schoolbooks, and hymnals, all cartwheel and rearrange like the stained glass slivers in a kaleidoscope. Farm work swallowed schooling when he was twelve. The humiliation of attempting to comprehend sticks and make sense out of circles was no great loss to Pastor Brother Sequoyah.

"Sir, I think you might have the wrong fellow..." Pastor Brother Sequoyah begins. The Spirit stretches out and thins itself into a bowl of living light over the Oconaluftee River.

The last thing Pastor Brother Sequoyah remembers is that glowing bowl scooping clear water out of the river and pouring it over his soul. When he comes to himself, he is stretched out on the same ground he walks now, worn-out like he's been in a struggle. Pastor Brother Sequoyah sits up and dusts himself off. Nothing has changed that he knows of, until he joins his mama and her sister Jeanietta at the settin-up for his great-uncle's wife, Margaret. The preacher from the Independent Baptist Church has been detained and the pastor from the Missionary Baptist Church has just finished his sermon on a woman named Martha, who gave The Lord an earful for running late when her brother died.

Tashina Alorha and Charli Rae get up and sing about where the roses never fade. Everybody shouts and waves their hands. Pastor Brother Sequoyah stuns himself by walking right up to the pulpit.

"Folks," Pastor Brother Sequoyah booms, in a voice that even he himself cannot recall hearing. He turns his head toward the Lord's Supper Table, where an oversized King James Bible stays open to the fifth chapter of St. Luke's Gospel. Pastor

Brother Sequoyah should not be able to read this. The fact that he does startles him.

Quickly, he shifts his stunned eyes toward a bulletin board declaring the number of students in Baptist Training Union, the number of Bibles brought, and the amount of the offering. The letters, the numbers mix and twist into an illegible jumble. Pastor Brother Sequoyah returns his gazed to the written-in-red passages of the Bible's thin pages. "I will, be clean," reads the crimson text. Pastor Brother Sequoyah can read. His amazement manifests in a full-bodied shout, which all the Missionary Baptists take as a sign of Holy Ghost salvation. Pastor Brother Sequoyah gets baptized and licensed in the same afternoon.

Pastor Brother Sequoyah reads nothing but the Bible. He announces this with great satisfaction, to anyone who will stop long enough to listen. That he can only read the King James 1611 version of the Bible serves to him and to others of his singular calling. Newspapers, The New International Version, and farm reports remain garbled, yet Pastor Brother Sequoyah reads through the minor prophets weekly. He is especially fond of Jonah, who warns folks to straighten up and fly right in a reasonable amount of space.

While Jesus Christ Himself commands His disciples to "go ye into all the world and preach the Gospel to every creature," Pastor Brother Sequoyah rarely has enough gasoline to get farther than the next county. For his intents and purposes, Pastor Brother Sequoyah decides, all the world means Cherokee, North Carolina. This is a sufficient mission field, Pastor Brother Sequoyah reasons, since it takes a day and an afternoon to cover on foot.

After all, these are his kin. Brother is his given name, the reward for being related to nearly every soul in Cherokee and the neighboring towns of Ela and Maggie Valley. The thought of close kin sweltering in eternal damnation settles it. When every soul in Cherokee is saved from the perils of Hell and other denominations, Pastor Brother Sequoyah will go into the rest of the world.

Tonight, Pastor Brother Sequoyah awakens suddenly. This is not unusual, except that Pastor Brother Sequoyah struggles to pray through. He tries, repeatedly, to seek God, to find Him in the middle of memorized Scriptures and remembered sermons.

"Say on, Sir," Pastor Brother Sequoyah pleads. He turns his head in Heaven's general direction. His neck creaks with the wear and tear of looking back. The moon, blood red round, fills the night sky. Pastor Brother Sequoyah watches the sky through irises glazed with the first blues of cataracts.

The stars are going out.

Pastor Brother Sequoyah gasps. He throws his hands upward. Gnarled fingers grasp at the constellations, as if to keep them lit a while longer.

"Lord, save us!" Pastor Brother Sequoyah hollers long and loud before realizing he has not made a sound.

"Ordinarily, I'd agree on that point," The Spirit standing before him says, "Only it's up to you this time. Get in the truck. Ain't got much time."

He's surprised to see the Spirit again and wonders if maybe it should drive. After all, he reasons, in matters of the Divine, it might be best not to lead, but to follow. He starts to offer to let The Spirit drive, until he looks over and sees that The Spirit is already riding shotgun.

Cherokee's farms yield to trees and hills. Pastor Brother Sequoyah crosses the state line into Tennessee, when The Spirit suddenly gestures for him to stop.

Pastor Brother Sequoyah skids into a stop by the roadside. Just right of the breakdown lane, an old Chevy has skidded into the ditch beside the highway. Brother Pastor Sequoyah inhales sharply. Under the Chevy's open door, a woman lies still. Cradled in her arms, a baby is blinking at him.

"Lord, have mercy," Pastor Brother Sequoyah moans. "Who are you, Usdi? Are you why the sky's falling?"

The baby blinks again. Pastor Brother Sequoyah stoops, his left knee popping like corn in sizzling oil. He reaches for the baby, trying to pry her from the dead woman's arms. Pastor Brother Sequoyah touches the cool flesh, which is smooth underneath his callused palm.

Pastor Brother Sequoyah considers going for help. He could get the highway patrol, who would investigate the situation. Only they might put the baby in foster care, where there would be no guarantee of a Baptist upbringing. Pastor Brother Sequoyah is not sure about transporting foundlings over state lines, and Vera Lo is not all the way up to walking the floors at night, what with her having asthma and all. He is weighing the issues and waiting for God to answer, when the baby's eyes begin to close.

"Come back," The Spirit shouts, "Come Back!"

The dead woman's eyes quicken into live orbs. They are round and shadowed with dark lashes. The baby yawns. Pastor Brother Sequoyah steps backward. The Spirit has knocked the wind out of him.

"Much obliged, Lord," he whispers.

"You're as welcome as you can be," The Spirit says. He bends over, and lifts the pair into the cab of Pastor Brother Sequoyah's truck. "Always watching out for widows and orphans. You can take it from here." The Spirit disappears as Pastor Brother Sequoyah climbs in beside the once-dead, now alive woman, and drives forward toward Cherokee.

Pastor Brother Sequoyah glances at his passengers. The woman sleeps deeply. So does the baby. Pastor Brother Sequoyah gazes at the night sky. For the first time in hours, it looks just fine.

ζ

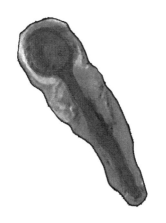

THE RATTLE

Amy Krout-Horn

Paulette Bordeaux's scissors lay on the dining room table, as if she were engaged in a sewing project. But the sewing machine was still in the corner. The beads for belt buckles and barrettes didn't litter the carpet. The hatband rawhide and porcupine quills weren't anywhere to be seen. Only the scissor, blades apart like a steel-beaked bird, was visible, and as if it had been hunting for nesting materials, the hinge rivet held a strand of hair.

Jack found his mother jostling dishes in the sink. Mumbling profanity, Paulette didn't acknowledge her son's arrival. The sound of cracking glass didn't faze her, either. Her seething surged on. Jack almost ushered a warning that she might cut her hand, but then remembered why he was home. In the shadowy hallway, his nephew, Seattle cowered. As the boy moved into the light, a thousand hot wires wrapped around Jack's gut. A familiar handprint reddened Seattle's cheek above a swollen lip, and bruised forearms. Flinching at what the boy held, Jack blinked, as if it might erase the image, but it fused with the past, the question Seattle had once asked, a playback loop in Jack's memory.

"Why did they cut their hair?"

That distant afternoon, Jack had turned to his nephew, who held an open book. The page contained a grainy photograph captioned "Carlisle Indian School new arrivals." At the dawn of the twentieth century, decades of costly warfare and removal to reservations, hadn't solved the US government's "Indian problem", so "Kill the Indian. Save the man" was conceived. But it wasn't men they sought for their sociological experiment. Through coercion and force, Native children were herded onto cattle cars and shipped to Pennsylvania.

Jack had seen the picture before; the uniforms, the boots, the boys' and girls' cropped hair. Everything familiar was stripped away, even their names; replaced with the "civilized" and "Christian."

There was an eerie resemblance between his nephew's pained incomprehension and that of the Carlisle students, and the room grew chilly, like ghosts had entered. Jack shivered as, one by one, they passed through him, and Seattle asked again, "Why?"

The stony look his nephew wore that afternoon, the afternoon they vowed to grow their hair long, was there now, -horror without tears.

Paulette whirled. Water flew off the spoon she held, and left an arch of droplets on the wall like blood spatters from a stabbing.

"I told you to stay in your room!" she bellowed.

Seattle focused on Jack, who stepped between them. In a voice too composed for what boiled within, he said, "Seattle, go pack."

Glaring, Paulette dropped the spoon. "What do you think you're doing?"

Jack moved towards her, every cell yearning to hurt her, but he heard the boy's startled breath, and resisted.

He told Seattle, "Don't worry. We're just going to talk."

Jack's monotone voice didn't align with his shakiness, but, trusting his uncle's non-violent history, Seattle retreated. Jack lowered to a whisper as he backed Paulette against the counter, and said, "Don't say anything. There isn't justification for what you've done. We're grown, so you hurt your grandson?"

Furiously, he shook his head, the long braid whipping forward, striking her.

"You've caused enough damage. You're done."

"You think you can snatch Seattle? I'm his guardian. I have rights."

Jack laughed, "You have rights? The right to beat him? The right to expose him to human garbage. Like the trash that raped his mother?"

Resisting, Paulette closed her eyes, but Jack's resentful landslide had momentum, and nothing could barricade it.

"Do you know how old I was the first time I saw you black out? I was three, Mom. I laid beside you and cried because I thought you were dead!"

He flipped his forearm, exposing cigarette burn scars.

"Here's your whiskey rages. All us kids got them, but that's nothing -compared to what you've done to our minds."

The counter dug into Paulette's spine, she shifted, but Jack's words kept pushing.

"And then there's Lily."

The name stuck in Jack's throat, grief's undertow threatening to drown him. Beautiful Lily, Seattle's fifteen-year old mother, dead at sixteen, heroin stilling her broken heart. He tread harder.

"Your rights? All you've got is wrongs."

Paulette's boozy breath nauseated him, and he walked away. She wound up for a rebuttal, but Jack spun. Gripping her fleshy shoulders, he backed her into the living room, and planted her on the sofa.

In the room he and Seattle shared, Jack threw clothes into a cardboard box. Seattle filled plastic bags. When you didn't have much, and could travel light, escape was easier. Their ancestors had known it; now they did, too.

"Where are we going, Uncle?"

"Some place better than this."

Seattle had never slept a night outside this room. Jack laid a hand on his head.

"I'll take care of you, Little Man. I promise."

As they passed, Paulette stood, but Jack hustled Seattle out the door. Wheezing heavily, she followed.

"It was nothing," she hollered. "The kid freaked over a God damn haircut."

Professor Augustus IronHorse saw Seattle and Jack emerge. A sweaty, red-faced woman stumbled out behind them.

"Paulette Bordeaux, I presume," IronHorse said under his breath, as he exited the Mustang.

As they approached, Gus couldn't stop his gaze from drifting towards Seattle's head or the way the sight dragged him back to his own troubled childhood.

Paulette staggered over, Gus intercepted, and Seattle crawled into the car.

"Who the hell are you?" she said with enough acidity that someone unfamiliar with her kind, might have recoiled, but Gus stayed put. "A social worker?"

"No, Ms. Bordeaux, I'm not–just a teacher and Jack's friend - but I do know one at Child Protective Services. Want me to call her?"

Paulette threw Jack a contemptuous look

"Go inside," Jack said. "We're leaving. I'll get Seattle's books later."

Paulette grunted, "The hell you will! I'll throw them away."

Apathy took hold; Jack opened the car door, and shrugged.

"Suit yourself."

Paulette's face flashed crimson crazy. Jack climbed in and IronHorse started the engine. As the Mustang pulled away, Paulette squatted, grabbed a crushed container off the ground, and hurled it. The trash slammed against the car window, a ketchup coated hamburger bun tumbled out, and slid down the glass like a bloody appendage.

Seattle clutched the severed ponytail, and licked the coppery taste of his lip. Would he ever see his grandmother again? The thought brought an odd convolution of relief and guilt. What if he hadn't sent the text message? What if Jack hadn't come home? When Seattle returned from school, Paulette had exploded, saying that he looked like a girl, that he needed a trim." When he protested, tried to explain, and then ran, she caught him, laughed, and said, "It's only hair." Was it? Maybe, if he hadn't pushed her away, she wouldn't have slapped him, wouldn't have grabbed his arms, or thrown him against the wall.

Paulette screamed, Seattle peered through the smeared window, and their eyes locked.

"You ungrateful bastards!" she roared over the 8-cylinder engine.

Seattle looked away. No, he thought. It's not just

hair.

Their exodus from Minneapolis, took them across the Mississippi, to IronHorse's St. Paul home. Barb StandingBull and their dog, Finnegan, were waiting on the front porch. Upon arrival, Gus looked at Barb, and she nodded. Beds were made up. Dinner for two was now dinner for four. A decade together taught them silent communication, and an imperceptible smile curled IronHorse's mouth. He tapped two fingers over his heart. She returned the gesture.

Behind Gus, Jack walked beside his nephew.

Gus said, "Remember Jack Bordeaux, my university teaching assistant?"

She nodded, offering a bright smile to the shy-looking boy next to him, saying, "You must be Seattle."

Without eye contact, the boy answered, and the old black lab stood, tail wagging.

"That's Finnegan," Gus said, seeing that the dog was assessing whether his arthritic legs could handle the porch steps. "I hope you like dogs because he loves kids."

Seattle crouched, offering a hand. Finnegan sniffed it, and then turned to Seattle's swollen lip. He smelled the bruises, the scratches, the length of hair in the boy's other hand, and then he licked Seattle's face, pressing himself into the boy's chest. Seattle hugged the retriever and cried.

Hesitantly, Barb touched Seattle's shoulder. At her feet, he dropped the hair and she recovered rubber band-bound, dark brown silk. StandingBull breathed in, restraining her anger, and as she did, she could smell shampoo and second-hand smoke.

She looked to IronHorse. Her jaw was granite, her eyes, fire. The question was written across both their faces. Who could do this to a child?

She said to the boy, "I'll keep this safe for you."

In a gritty whisper, Seattle said, "Thank you."

At twilight, they gathered in the back yard. Barb carried a trowel. Jack brought IronHorse's tobacco pouch. Gus held the ceremonial pipe, and Seattle gripped the foot-long bundle of hair. Where lavender iris bloomed, Barb turned over the rich earth, and when the shallow hole was dug, she laid a red prayer tie inside. She then looked to Seattle. He stared first at the hair and then, the spot of disrupted ground, until at last, unable to lay it in the resting place, he offered it to Barb.

As she arranged the strands around the prayer tie, Seattle closed his eyes. He heard the trowel scraping earth and Barb's voice whispering a Lakota prayer, and as he listened, his thoughts turned inward, towards something, someone, that he rarely allowed himself to contemplate. Seattle thought of his mother.

At midnight, wind swept through an open window into the room where Seattle slept. It caressed him, leaving tear-like raindrops on his skin, and he sighed. Lightning illuminated the snapshot that lay on the bed table. Frozen in time, a blue-eyed young woman gazed down, away from the camera, her beauty immortalized. Another gale sent the picture swirling. Thunder shook window glass. Seattle slumbered on, safe within a dream of a turtle, white owls, and women dancing.

In the blackness, their talons scratched cottonwood bark, and the unsettling sound caused Barb StandingBull to look up at the branches. Lightning veins lit pairs of huge amber eyes and ghostly-white faces. Something cold ran its finger along Barb's spine. Another brilliant flash struck, but the glowing round eyes above didn't blink. A dream? Barb thought. Yes, I am dreaming them.

But the grass felt wet, the ozone, too acrid, and the eerie inquisition, "Who? Who? Who?" clearly echoed.

The storm strengthened, wind wailed, and the spectral chorus's feathers rippled. Suddenly, a young woman appeared from behind the cottonwood's massive trunk. She wore the dress of the ancients; deerskin adorned with Ojibwe porcupine quillwork. Her waist-length hair brushed the belt of deer's teeth encircling her hips. She walked towards Barb. Wind tossed the dark brown mane across the young woman's blue eyes and rattled the belt's pine needle stained teeth. Mystified, Barb spoke her name. But the young woman only smiled and opened a hand. A turtle sat there, its head thrust forward. Barb watched the creature, until its black eyes gleamed. From beneath its shell, White beams shimmered. The light grew almost blinding, as the reptile drew its head and legs in. Barb's heart beat slow, but strong, and the young woman knowingly nodded. She then closed her fingers around the turtle and the light vanished. When she again opened them, the animal, too, was gone. In its place, sat a rattle, the top half turtle shell, and the lower, synched raw hide. Another electric flash ripped the sky, exposing the crimson outline of a heart painted on the shell's center. Like sunrays, lines of white pigment bled from its red borders.

The young woman cupped the object and shook it in a slow steady rhythm. As she did, the rain fell with greater force, the wind roared with more ferocity, and suddenly, Barb became aware that her own hands weren't empty. She offered what she held to the young woman, who accepted it. For a moment, their fingers met, icy mist against warm flesh. The young woman then pivoted and began to dance, her feet keeping time with the rattle, and as she moved in a circle, she gestured for StandingBull to follow. Rain fell in torrents, drenching their hair and the hair that the young woman carried, hair identical in color to her own, and they danced. It soaked Barb's nightgown and splashed around her bare feet, and they danced. Lightning connected heaven to Earth, and the women danced. They danced and danced, until the rain was blurred glass between them. Then the young woman and the owls fused with the water and the wind, and with the force of their departure, Barb StandingBull collapsed.

Somewhere, a dog barked. Someone shouted her name. Barb's lids fluttered. Suddenly, strong arms lifted her from the drenched earth.

"Wake up!" Gus yelled.

He shook her, something falling from her fingers. Struggling away, she groped the grass for it, but he pulled Barb to her feet. He carried her to the house, where Finnegan yowled. He deposited her onto the kitchen floor, and the dog licked rainwater from her ankles. Gus stripped off her clothes, brought a robe, and gently toweled her hair.

"What were you doing out there?"

Though dazed, she knew what had transpired, but she couldn't find the words. A Lakota elder had once said that their people had, before the arrival of Christianity and the English language, possessed secret words, known only to the wisest medicine people, Words uttered to relate the greatest aspects of their mysticism. Somehow, she sadly knew that this story would have best been told in that lost tongue.

Sitting across from her, Gus cupped Barb's cold hands and said, "I woke up because Finnegan was at the back door, going crazy, and I couldn't find you. It scared the hell out of me. I thought you were gone."

."I don't think that anyone ever really is gone, -just in the elsewhere," said Barb.

Gus looked perplexed.

"I was two places; out there," she said, turning

her head towards the door, "and in the elsewhere. It's wakan. It's sacred. That's all I know. Trust me."

The rain stopped and the steady "blup blup blup" of water dripping into the rain barrel, slowed.

As he stroked Barb's fingers, something Grandpa IronHorse once told him, returned.

"We don't always have to seek a vision; sometimes it finds us."

"I trust you," Gus said.

In early dawn's indigo, with all but the morning star faded, Barb heard scratching, and crawled from beneath IronHorse's embrace. Finnegan pawed the back door, and she unlocked the screen, stepping out behind him. She inhaled the clean, green smell of the rain-washed world. Where spirit owls had perched, robins now stirred. Grandma Daisy taught her that they are the first birds to greet the day, and the last to bid it farewell. Her grandmother had taught her many things: hand-stitching, spring potato planting, and old Lakota songs. Grandma Daisy had also taught about naji.

"White folks call them ghosts. They scare each other with stories about how they haunt houses, rattling chains and breaking dinner plates," she told her grandchildren. "I don't know about those naji. I just know about our kind."

"What do our naji do?" Barb had asked.

"When they visit from the spirit world, it's for something important. Sometimes, there are things they need to do here before they can be peaceful.

They want to help a loved one in this world, and only the naji have powerful enough medicine. So they meet us in the elsewhere and bring the pejuta wakan, the sacred medicine."

As Barb stood in the sweet perfume of fresh lilacs, Finnegan came to her side. He whined, pressing his damp muzzle against her leg, until she squatted and asked, "What is it?"

The dog dropped something at her feet, and it issued a strangely familiar sound. She reached into the wet grass and retrieved a rattle; a rattle with a painted heart and white lines; a rattle made from a turtle's shell.

Seattle Bordeaux stood in the kitchen doorway. Late Morning sun spilled around him, puddling at his edges, framing a miracle, and he waited for someone to notice. Jack turned from the table first, and stammered his nephew's name as both question and exclamation. Over Seattle's shoulders, down his chest, lay long beautiful strands of healthy hair.

Barb and Gus registered Jack's shock and looked the boy's direction. Seattle gently tugged the hair, saying, "It's real."

For a breath, no one spoke. Seattle's lip still bore a cut. A purplish bruise marked his cheek. Except for the inexplicable mane of hair, the proof of Paulette's attack remained.

"When I woke up, it was there," Seattle said, pulling the photograph from a pocket. " And this was on the pillow beside me."

Jack took the snapshot; the only remaining picture of his sister, the only one Seattle had of his mother. IronHorse looked to Barb. She was crying. Seattle spoke.

"I thought about her yesterday; when we buried my hair, while Barb was praying, I thought about my..."

The word always felt like a piece of broken tooth, something that belonged to him, but because of trauma or neglect or weakness, had cracked loose. Though he wanted to spit it out, doing so was the ultimate admission that reattachment was impossible.

"Your mother," said Jack.

Seattle nodded and said, "She was in my dream last night, flying through a storm, with White owls. Then she danced, -with a turtle in her hand."

Shaking, Barb stood. She went to Seattle, lifting something from her skirt's deep pocket.

"My dream," said the boy, when she placed the rattle in his hand.

"Mine, too," Barb replied.

Adapted from the novel, Dancing in Concrete Moccasins

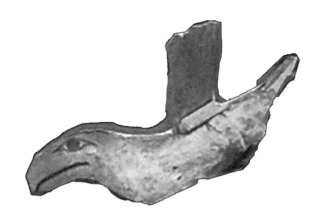

Blessings from a Bird

Evan Pritchard

I was rushing off to work when I received a phone call from a highly respected Native American elder from West Virginia named Running Deer. She told me that my long-time friend Blessing Bird had passed away. A fatal disease that she had held hidden from me and in some ways from herself for many years had finally overcome her. She died on October 3rd, 2011.

The news came as quite a shock, and I immediately felt as if half of me had been transported to some region of the spirit world I had not been to before. That half was experiencing a kind of otherworldly bliss, while the half that stayed behind was slowing sinking into sorrow.

I had been working on the book *Bird Medicine: The Secret Power of Bird Shamanism*, and was about to finalize the manuscript for Inner Traditions. Blessing Bird had been on my mind, as she had been a wonderful source of material throughout the process. I had been sending her copyright release forms and was getting concerned that I had not heard back. I had known Blessing Bird for at least 20 years, and though it took a while to get to know her, I was glad when we began to correspond regularly. She was happy to have me drop by unexpectedly to read through the varied collection of Native American books in her personal library, and have some tea. Her unfinished book all about spiders in Native American lore was one of several hints I received from spirit to write a book just about birds. She turned out to be a rich source of bird stories.

After resting the receiver back in its cradle, I sighed a breath of sorrow and had to sit down. I had to compose myself before driving the long and stressful ride into the suburbs of New York City. I set out on my sorrowful journey to work, along the hectic racecourse of Taconic Parkway, thinking and wondering about Blessing Bird, and little else. Just north of Ossining, New York, where the lanes become divided as they cut through rock, and driving 55 miles per hour, the posted speed limit, I watched in amazement as a large female red-tailed hawk positioned herself right outside my driver's side window, which was closed. The end of her right wingtip was less than a foot from my window and she was gliding effortlessly at the same speed

I was traveling, navigating a narrow passage between a cliff-like embankment to her left and me to her right.

I had a car positioned to my right as well, as I was in the passing lane, but it was hard to keep my eyes on the road. Then the bird swooped down and sped along with me, gliding six inches to a foot off the ground so that I could see the somewhat symmetrical pattern of rust red and white triangles on her back and head, close up. I felt as if I were flying with her. After what seemed like an eternity, she rose up again, flying beside me again at eye level but just to the fore, looking straight ahead. The cliff ended. She slowed down to let me catch up to her, and then suddenly turned her head directly toward me and stared at me from about two feet away. I went into a trance. In all my adventures with birds, I had never experienced anything like that before.

I remembered I was driving a car but could not remember where I was going. I turned my eyes back to the road for a single second. Everything was fine, but my exit was approaching, across traffic. When I looked back at the hawk again, she rose up and flexed one wing tip in the universal "bird salute" gesture. It was unmistakable. Then she threw her head back in the equally unmistakable "see you around" gesture, all of which flowed beautifully together as only a hawk can do. Then she shot off into the woods. If that wasn't Blessing Bird traveling inside that bird to say hello from the spirit world, I'd like to hear a better explanation. I guess she really wanted to be in that book!

Running Deer had said that it was among Blessing Bird's last requests that her stories be included in Bird Medicine. Few elders have the "Bird Medicine" gift like our young Blessing Bird had; she was truly one with them. Of course, her request has been granted, and a copy of *Bird Medicine* was donated to the memorial library and Native American resource center, which is being built in Jackson, West Virginia, in her honor.

It was truly a blessing from a bird, and a visit from the spirit world as well, one that I shall never forget.

JACKALOPE STARTS A MEMOIR

Denise Low

Jack swallows a blast of high-octane coffee and sets down the mug. He looks at the blank page again and types the opening, "Once upon a time when Rabbit was tramping along," and stops. Should he tell the story like he remembers or like it is written in books? "Tramping" is such an odd verb and does not really capture the reference to Rabbit's episodic lifestyle. Oh, well. He is on deadline, and the old ethnographic version is easiest.

Jack continues the story as the books tell it, "Rabbit saw some kind of creature flying 'round aloft."

The spiraling of birds, however, is not really "flying 'round aloft." The term "kettling" is more accurate, but obscure. Jack pauses a moment, then types, "Rabbit looked up and saw a lordly bird circling the morning sunrise." That sounds better. Jack continues, "Rabbit was bedazzled by its feather cape." Good, Jack thinks. The cape illustrates the elegant feather garments once worn throughout the Americas.

"Whoosh!"

Jack startles and freezes as he hears rustling in the dark corner of his basement office. He turns, but nothing is there. Maybe a mouse. He turns back to the screen and rereads what he has written. He sees a possible problem. "Lordly," is not a very Indigenous American word, with references to European caste systems. The old book's description is simply "lordly," so he embellishes, "The plumes shimmered all colors of the rising sun." Now Jack can see the prism of colors in his mind.

"Whoosh." Again, he hears a rustling, like wind seeping in the edges of windows, but his office has none. He is not frightened by the odd sounds but they do put him on edge. He waits a few heartbeats, but silence returns.

He looks back at the screen, "The plumes shimmered all colors of the rising sun," and he finishes the sentence, "as the bird spiraled high in the heavens, close to the sun, moon, planets, and stars."

There. This takes care of the "flying 'round aloft" part, references the more familiar Icarus story for non-Indigenous readers, and leads right to the trickster conflict. He types, "Rabbit envied the bird for its beautiful, flashing feathers, so unlike his own dirty-socks-colored fur." Jack looks down at his own bare, muddy feet on the floor and the grimy socks next to them. Okay, yes, he could be a humble trickster type himself. He just needs some better attention from the helpful spirits, not just rattles in a corner, but hey, he isn't complaining. Back to the topic and no more attention deficit meanders.

"Rabbit envied the bird's ability to fly," continues Jack on the page," and he envied its charisma. Indeed, he wanted the bird's gifts for himself."

Okay, now for some dialogue. He is starting to hear the characters' voices, now, especially a wheezy narrator who dictates to him, as he types, "Rabbit called up." Then Jack hears another voice speak Rabbit's dialogue, "'Hey, hey!' to the beautiful sky being. 'Please give me a ride on your back!'" That sounds just like nephew Fuzzy's wheedling tone. Good.

Another whoosh comes from the corner, but Jack ignores it. He pulls out the Bloomsbury's Menominee Texts again to look at the original story, a bit different from the one he heard from his grandmother. He flips through the pages.

"Jack!" Suddenly, Grandmother Koko calls from the kitchen, "Jack Kelley Lamat, where are you!" Her voice is in imperative overdrive.

"Be there in a minute," he says. He saves the

file "Rabbit_Buzzard" and drops it in a folder, "Jackalope Texts." More rustling, like a large bird roosting, comes from the corner, but spirits and everyone must stand aside for Grandmother.

"Jack!"

"On my way." He smells savory spinach frying in olive oil with garlic. Mmm. He is not sorry to be interrupted. As they eat dinner, he can ask Grandma to repeat the Rabbit story like she heard it from her elders, and she will make it come to life. Lightning and thunder will arise at the part about creation. They both will cry at the sad losses. Buzzard will pay for his high-flying hubris. Rabbit will triumph.

No matter how hard he tries, Jack cannot make his typed letters do anything more than flicker shadows of the mesmerizing tales Grandmother tells at the kitchen table. He can only raise a few flutters from spirits lost in his basement.

Denise Low's book of short prose is *Jackalope* (Red Mountain Press 2016). "Jackalope Starts a Memoir" is a new episode in the hero/heroine's ongoing journey.

PÁL MÍYAXWE TÍNGAYPISH

Water is Medicine
Sean Milanovich

Just outside the ceremony, the fall equinox was in procession. The crescent moon rested above the ridge of the mountain. The people gathered to honor the celestial event. The stars glistened in the night sky. *Wánewet* or the Milky Way captured the viewers' attention as it streamed north to south. The night was cold but the ceremony in the teepee was warm. The all night ceremony brought the people together for prayer and healing. Like many other ceremonies, the ancestral spirits spoke about water; they often spoke about the sanctity of water when they visited. Even the ceremony itself involved the acknowledgment of water as medicine

The ceremony was on the ancestral land of the *Wánakik* Cahuilla, the original occupants around *Tákusk Héki* or San Jacinto Mountain in California. The *Wánakik* are one of several bands of Cahuilla Indians that continue to reside within their homelands today. The name *Wánakik* originates from the word *wánish* or stream. *Pál* or water is essential to all life. The Cahuilla developed a relationship with water since time immemorial. Cahuilla acknowledge and honor all water bodies including springs, rivers, oceans, clouds and underground sources. The Cahuilla have learned water heals the people and the land.

The *á'avuwetem* or ancestors gave a message that night during the ceremony to an individual called by the children *Pá'at* meaning bighorn sheep. *Pá'at* loved to hike in the mountains as do bighorn sheep. The message *Pá'at* received was to visit all the sacred water bodies including the Colorado River. The ancestors said the Cahuilla used to journey to the river to offer prayers. The water bodies are living entities and need love, the ancestors declared. *Pá'at* was instructed to sing and feed the water. The ancestors told him to sing and offer prayers to local springs. Trips to the Colorado River and the Pacific Ocean were required to carry out the prayer. *Pá'at* wondered aloud when was the last time someone visited the Colorado River to offer prayers.

During the ceremony, the ancestors presented *Pá'at* with a vision or a story of a local spring down the mountain. He saw in his vision a clump of dried palms tucked away into the dunes. This spring had dried up a long time ago. Surrounded by many palms and mesquite, the spring previously supported a village of native people. The people loved their home and the spring that fed them. Children ran through the trees and crawled through the thickets playing games. The people conducted ceremonies around the spring and used it for healing and travel. But then a new group of people came into the area that threatened the Indians' way of life. Soldiers exterminated the Indians that occupied the spring. The massacre killed all but one who escaped with his daughter. A horrible event had happened and the spring was alone. No one came to sing to the spring anymore. The spring was sad. The spring slowly receded below the surface waiting for others to return some day.

Pá'at was instructed to visit the spring. Numerous palms and tamarisks trees cluster around the area today. The ancestors said the spring was alive – that the water was still present but had gone underground. They told *Pá'at* if he and others sang and offered prayers to the spring, it would flow again. He understood the message. That morning leaving from ceremony *Pá'at* went to give offerings at two springs. He offered flowers and song.

This prayer is the beginning of a relationship to revitalize the community and was started long ago when the ancestors laid down the prayer asking someone to come and acknowledge the water. Water is medicine. The Cahuilla Creation Story helps to understand where this idea of water is medicine comes from and gives the Cahuilla worldview.

ς

In the beginning, all was darkness and still. There was no earth. Two forces of energy - *Amna'a*, the prominence of all things and *Túkmiat* the night - traveled across the vast emptiness of the cosmos. The two forces came together. *Amna'a* and *Túkmiat* wrapped around each other and created two embryos. The embryos grew rapidly. Two boys were born into the darkness and floated in space. They quarreled about who was older. The older brother *Múkat* wanted to clear his mind and focus his thoughts. He reached into his heart and pulled out his pipe. His brother *Témayawet* did the same. The brothers reached into their hearts, pulled out tobacco and loaded their pipes. They smoked their pipes and blew the smoke in the four directions.
The two brothers *Amna'a* and *Túkmiat* knew what to do. They would create *témal*, the earth. First, *Amna'a* and *Túkmiat* reached into their hearts, pulled out the *húyanawet*

or sacred staff. The staff used as a center pole, gave strength, foundation and balance to the earth. *Amna'a* and *Túkmiat* then reached into their hearts, pulled out black and white earth, and molded the earth around the staff. The earth was uneven. *Múkat* and *Témayawet* reached into their hearts and pulled out creatures. Spiders and ants spread the earth smooth. *Múkat* and *Témayawet* both reached into their hearts again and pulled out water. The water covered most of the earth. *Múkat* and *Témayawet* reached into hearts once more and placed sacred beings into the oceans, rivers and springs. These creatures created a balance of good and bad.

Afterwards, the twin brothers created *táwlistem* or people. They pulled black and white earth from their hearts and created man. *Múkat* and *Témayawet* blew air into their mouths giving them life. *Múkat* gave the people everything they needed. The people gathered and circled the earth three times before settling where they are now.

ζ

Water is a sacred space. Many American Indians believe springs are underground spiritual highways that are connected and that all springs are connected. One can enter a spring in Palm

Springs, California and come out in a spring in Eugene, Oregon. The springs specifically are an underground highway to the spirit world. Supernatural beings dwell deep below the surface in cavernous chambers. They are not spirits of the dead. These beings are there to help the people that need and want healing.

Medicine men gained access to the *Núkatem*, the Cahuilla supernatural beings from the spring. On the Agua Caliente Reservation, deep within the spring, *Séxi* or Boiling Water, there lived these beings in a dry room. Some call them *pál'akniwatem* or water babies. There lived a white deer, a blue frog, a red racer, a mountain lion and a baby indicated Francisco Patenci, *Nét* or hereditary clan chief of the *Kówisictem* Cahuilla. Francisco was also a *púl* or medicine man. The *púl* traveled down into the spring to visit the *Núkatem* and ask for help. The medicine men prayed for help for the people there within the spring. The healing they received was the power of the spring itself.

The Cahuilla Indians have a long history of using the spring for healing and power and using the springs for medicine continues today. Agua Caliente tribal member Sean Milanovich broke his right hip a few years ago. The doctors told him he would never walk again. His right leg had no feeling. His father Richard Milanovich, Tribal Chairman, knew of the healing properties of the spring. Richard took his son Sean to the hot spring to soak in the hot mineral waters and visit with the spirits there. Within a month of soaking in the mineral water, Sean regained feeling in his leg. Soon, he was walking. Sean contributed his healing to the powerful spring and to *Núkatem* that resided there. He honors the spring with food and song. Sean contributes his ability to walk today directly to the spring.

Others like Kaweah Red Elk said she goes to sit in the spring water to pray for healing. Kaweah lives in Colorado but has ties to Agua Caliente. One of her grandfathers is Francisco Lugo who was one of the first recorded inhabitants at Agua Caliente. Red Elk said she comes to pray with her pipe. She feeds the spring tobacco and songs from her heart. Kaweah says she has traveled using the spring. Kaweah understands the power of the spring and knows it can help the people if they ask. William Pink, a Cupeño and close relative of the Cahuilla agreed all springs are connected. Respected for his traditional knowledge of plant use, William knows much about the history of Southern California Indians and their spiritual connections. He allured most of the rock art in Southern California is associated with water. The rock art is often located at a source of water.

There is one special place up West Fork Canyon on the reservation. This place is located within the river channel of a perennial streambed. The water over time has cut through the rock exposing a wall of granite. Long ago, the *Mómopechem* pecked onto the granite wall a series of rock art panels. The panels are rectangular and have a maze pattern. This was Tribal Chairman Richard Milanovich's favorite spot in the entire San Jacinto range. Needles Eye was the place where he came to clear his mind and walk with a good heart. He became one with the water and the land. Richard said this place allowed him to be. The place was soothing and yet energizing. It left one feeling invigorated and ready to move forward in a positive way. Many ask what the rock art here represents. Some say the etchings are unknown. Others hint to boundary markers. Yet, others say the mazes here are portals to the spirit world.

Many people used the springs in traditional times to travel from one place to another. Today, the people use the same springs to travel from place to place on spiritual journeys. Many Cahuilla elders say Stories and Legends, as told by Francisco Patencio are true. There are people today whom have traveled and use the springs to travel as mentioned by Francisco. Springs are a doorway to access the *Núkatem*. Messages sent through the springs aided the people in places far away. *Pá'at* once traveled during ceremony through the springs. He entered *Séxi* and came out at another doorway in Palm Canyon. *Pá'at* has since traveled through many springs and portals.

There are many stories about hot springs that show the connection with the people of long ago. Some stories tell of the origin of springs. For *Séxki* or the home of the Agua Caliente Band of Cahuilla

Indians, the tribe gets its name from the hot springs there called *Séxi*. The spring created long ago was a sign for the migrating people to settle in the area. *Yéwi* or long ago, *Tomiyat Me'um* or Sungrey, one of the original five headmen, came through the area now known as Palm Springs. He was tired after looking for a place for his people to settle. He sat down and admired the mountains that surrounded him. He must have felt something special for this place, for what he did next changed the scene for generations to follow. Sungrey stood tall and firm. He thrust his sacred staff of leadership into the ground causing the earth to open a little. Hot water came to the surface and has since flowed. Sungrey entered the water to revive and heal his exhausted body.

When the first people settled around the spring, the power and the creative force they possessed was unknown. The people were afraid. This was the case at *Séxi*. The *múluwetem* or the first ones were scared to go near the spring. The spring had a solid grove of mesquite growing around it. The people heard noises. Some heard babies crying. These were the water babies. One day, the sound of a crying baby lured three sisters close to the spring. They crawled through the thickets and could see a white baby in the water crying. The youngest of the sisters went to grab the baby. A *ténanqa* or whirlwind blew nearby. It sucked the young girl and baby up into the air and then took them both into the spring. The older sisters ran away. The girl's father, a medicine man came that evening and prayed. The next morning, the girl's body floated to the surface. The people gathered in the *Kíshumnawet* or Ceremonial House, offered gifts, and prayed to the spring. The people developed a relationship with the water. The people soon bathed and played in the water freely and asked for help when needed.

There are many stories about springs and their importance. There is the story of *Táhow Tésnekish* or Yellow Body. Long ago, one of the five headmen who settled in the middle of Cahuilla territory at a place called *Pánoxsu*. He had strong medicine and lived a long time with his dog and many wives over the years. He often went into the spring water there to rejuvenate his tired old body into a young man. He remarried many times. After much time, Yellow Body knew his time was coming and he too would pass. He took his dog and mother-in-law with him. They crossed Borrego Valley. There is a hot spring on the other side of the *Wílum'mo* or Santa Rosa Mountains called *Kúpa*. There in the spring, Yellow Body took out a large basket and all three got in. The spring began to swirl around and swallowed up Yellow Body and his family forever. *Kúpa* - meaning to drink - gets its name from this event. The spring drank up Yellow Body and his family.

Southern California Indians established villages and camps at springs and water troughs. Consistently, the individuals and families settled at springs to enjoy the refreshing water they provided. The California Indians also enjoyed the economy the water brought. The Creator knew this and actually placed springs to help the people thrive and coexist amongst one another. In Southern California, east of Los Angeles out in the dry Mojave and Colorado Deserts, lie ancient trails of the original inhabitants: Cahuilla, Chemehuevi, Cupeño, Luiseno, Serrano, and the Tongva. The natives created a great expansive trade network weaving through the web of springs. The springs allowed the people to travel and rest up along the way. One spring, Corn Springs surrounded with hundreds of rock art panels, lies on a worn beaten trail. The people planted corn there, rested and had ceremony.

Certain families resided at some of the springs. The families cared for the travelers along the way. The Pine Family that lived at the Oasis of *Már'rah* in the Mojave Desert traded chia seeds to the people that traveled from the oceans acquiring shells and tar pitch while those who traveled from the Colorado River traded corn and beans. *Már'rah* was a busy place. The spring was a place of importance to all who came upon it. *Máulem* or palm trees surround *Már'rah*. The traders and travelers brought the palms to the springs. The palms provided food, shelter, clothing and basket material. The palms also signaled to the migrating people that water was ahead. The Pine Family and later the Mike Family were the last Indian caretakers of the spring.

Guided by the ancestors, *Pá'at* visited the once whirling spring and offered prayers and food establishing the connection. He had been here many times before, although this time was different. He knew he needed to visit the Colorado River soon as instructed by the ancestors. *Pá'at* was soon to lead a group of people on a camping trip out to the Old Woman Mountain Preserve where there was a beautiful rock art site and a cave that happened to be next to a spring. *Pá'at* thought he might be able to visit the river after and the trip.

Within two weeks, *Pá'at*, his family and friends went to the Old Women Mountains. There the adults and children learned about the plants and the spiritual connection with water. The cave was located next to a spring and well hidden. The spring had bees, an indicator of the spirit world. Only those with permission had access. There was another portal on a rock panel nearby. *Pá'at* was troubled with returning the people on time and yet he was on a mission to visit the river. The ancestors opened some doors and *Pá'at* was asked to take the people to the Colorado River after the camping trip. Five trucks filled with Indians journeyed through the desert on dirt roads. They followed in procession en route to the Colorado River as their ancestors had done millennia before. Matt Leivas, a Chemehuevi elder lead the group. Matt ultimately gave access to the river from the Colorado River Indian Reservation. Upon arriving at Lake Havasu, Leivas told the group about the deer and bighorn sheep that used to swim across the river. These animals are powerful spiritual beings.

Pá'at gave prayers, songs and tobacco to the ancient Colorado River. He acknowledged the great water body and the animals and people that used it. *Pá'at* said thank you to the ancestors who helped him on this journey. In celebration, Clemencia and Maria cooked a feast that afternoon on the banks of the great Colorado. The children played. Some ventured out into the water. The ancestors told *Pá'at* it was the not the prayer that was important but the journey that was taken to get to that point. Prayers laid down generations ago culminated that day. It was about making a connection to the water, understanding the responsibility and securing the water for future generations. Water is Family.

ح

SPIRITS R US

William S. Yellow Robe, Jr.

We had just returned from this all day "Shaman's Working and Aura Exploration Workshop." Lisa, who had been with me for about a year, had saved nearly two thousand dollars to attend this gathering. I helped out by pitching in fifteen hundred dollars, plus airfare, hotel, and vegan meals. What can I say? It made her happy. I opened the door and noticed all this powder on the floor. "Lisa," I called, "there's all this white powder on the carpet."

"I know," she said, "I'm testing to see if we have any spirits in the house."

"Are they coke head spirits," I asked, "or do they just need a cleansing?"

"No, but look down and see if you see any foot prints," she said.

I tossed my small suitcase on the couch. I turned on the light and looked around. Nothing. But what is that near the edge of the carpet? There were these three little triangle marks, forming a large triangle, right at the edge of the carpet. "What 'a my looking for Lisa?"

"Foot prints."

"Like a dog, or cat?"

"Yeah, those are cool, but if it has three claws it means it is an inhuman spirit."

"Inhuman? Like the guy who was leading the drumming circle at the gathering?"

"No. Like in devil, or demon."

I looked closely at the three triangles. It could be a print, but it could also be her new clogs she wore on the airplane. I looked around the couch and the chairs, underneath the coffee table, lifted a lamp, a few magazines, and wondered what had happened to the cat.

"Okay Lisa, come in now," I said. I just thought had I not said anything she would have remained out in the hallway for the next half hour. When she came inside she brushed her shiny auburn hair to the side. I remember now why I would do anything for her. Her green eyes were so bright. Unlike some people who are mixed blood, or of Indian ancestry, she never tried to get colored lenses to make her eyes darker. It would have shamed us out if she had.

"I'm going straight to bed, Babe," she said as she took her rolling bag, three paper bags, and two plastic shopping bags to the bedroom. Her dress made a little cloud of dust rise as she walked across the carpet. Half way across she kicked off her lime green clogs and they came to a landing near the coffee table. Her feet nearly disappeared into the powder and for some strange reason I thought that was kind of weird, but in a good way, because it was her.

"You're not going to stay up and watch your show?"

"No, I'm going to use this energy and get a good night's sleep. Come in when you are ready."

"All right," I said. "Damn, bummer," is what I said to myself. Sleeping that night was sort of easy. I drifted right off to sleep. I held Lisa with my right arm, with my left side of my head on the pillow, and an old quilt covering both of us. Then, for some strange reason, in my dream, there was a big opening in the blackness of sleep and I moved forward. I didn't know where I was. I looked around and could see stars above me, but my feet were standing on something. Stone? I'd never felt anything like this floor, or was it ground? I don't know what it was. I raised my foot and tried to stomp on it waiting to hear a sound, or to feel the pain of my bare foot making contact, but there was nothing. No sound.

"Damn. Am I dead?" I asked aloud as panic raced through my mind. I realized I heard my question so I wasn't dead. Then I thought, but if you are dead, you are the only one who can hear your words because you are dead. And if you are dead, then why are you talking to yourself? Shouldn't there be an angel or spirit about now I should be talking with? Or maybe Death showing up and we have a rousing game of chess? I looked around and saw nothing.

"I said, 'Am I dead?' " Again, I waited.

"No." said a voice.

"Who, who, are you?"

"Can't see us yet?" said the voice.

"Why would he ask if he could see us when he clearly can't see us?" said another voice.

"Let's sort this out then," a third voice said. There was a loud screeching noise. I covered my ears and held on to my head with all my might. I nearly closed my eyes when all of a sudden there was light from a fire, but I couldn't see any flame. I slowly lowered my arms exposing my ears. And there they were. Standing just ten feet away from me.

A large green dragon, shiny like jade in sunlight, sitting on its hind legs as it propped its front half upward and moved its head side to side with quick, sharp movements. The talons of the dragon's claws were bright red, glowing like red crystal, or deeper, like rubies. A griffin, made up of part lion, a serpent's tail, and part duck -yeah, duck- stood near the dragon. The tail of the griffin whipped across the floor in long motions like a fireman's hose. Very scary to watch from a close distance but it didn't frighten me. What did frighten me was when it opened its mouth there were all these razor sharp teeth like a great white shark. No more shark week on TV for me, I thought.

The third animal present was a small hedgehog. It looked like a small pincushion standing next to the other two animals. "Now, can you see us?" asked the hedgehog.

"Yeah, uh, how, what is going on?" and once I asked this I wondered if I should have a weapon or something.

"No need for weapons," said the dragon as it moved to the left and I countered the dragon's move. I don't know why because if the dragon attacked the only thing I could do was become a nice Indian snack for it.

"You are a member of the gathering of humans who called us," said the griffin.

"Gathering?" Oh. I knew then! The workshop on summoning your spirit guide animals! I had attended the workshop so I could be next to Lisa who was wearing just a tank top and that red skirt. I loved watching her when she dressed semi-hippie.

"Yes," said the hedgehog that had a leaf of lettuce in his little paws and began chewing.

"I didn't call you, it wasn't me," I said.

"Didn't you request for direction and asked for a spirit animal to be summoned to aid you in your quest for clarity and vision?" The dragon shifted a little, puffed up its chest and produced a small cloud of smoke from its nostrils.

"No, I..." I began to have a coughing fit. Man, dragon smoke is harsh. "It, it, I...no, not me."

"Are you quite sure?" asked the griffin.

"Yes," I said, "if I needed help from a spirit animal, I'd call one of my relatives."

"Ah, see, I knew it wasn't him," said the griffin.

"Then why are we here?" The dragon poured out a little more smoke.

"Who said it was him? Maybe someone asked for him," said the hedgehog.

"You mean someone asked for me," I looked at all three. "That means, no, I don't think Lisa would have done that."

"Let's eat him and go," said the dragon.

"No," the hedgehog and I said together.

"Well, we have to do something since he's seen us," said the griffin.

"We are here to help and to advise," said the hedgehog.

"Right, let's eat him and go on to the next request," said the dragon.

"No!"

The dragon started to move in a half circle around me. The griffin was shifting its weight from front to back legs. I think it was ready to take flight. "Do any of you remember the request?" asked the hedgehog. "It said to remove the thing that was holding back the person who was making the request," said the griffin.

"Yes," said the dragon," to remove the burden of the person's life. So they could have a better life."

"Lisa? Lisa told you guys that?"

"We can't reveal that to you since you aren't the person who requested our services. It wouldn't be acceptable," said the hedgehog.

"Wait, wait," I screamed, "how can you folks harm me when you aren't even part of my reality, whether it be dream, spirit, or earthly bound reality?"

"Good point," said the hedgehog as he looked at the other two animals.

"No, it isn't," said the griffin.

"Eat and leave, I say," said the dragon.

"He obviously loves the person who made the request," said the hedgehog.

"How do you know that," asked the dragon, "the request was to remove a burden. He looks like a right sized burden, if you ask me."

"Yes, how do you know he loves her?" The griffin was now pacing.

"I spent two hundred dollars on all those tinctures," I said, "and I bought her all those ground herbs."

"He has wealth. What does he offer us?" The dragon became still.

"We wouldn't be doing this if there were more requests," said the griffin.

"And I didn't request you," I said.

"We're not here for you," said the dragon.

"Do you love the person who requested us?" The hedgehog moved forward to me.

"Who, who was it?"

"The person who summoned us and made the request is a maiden called Sarah," said the hedgehog.

"Who the hell is that?" I asked.

"See! Let's eat and leave! He doesn't know her!" said the dragon.

Sarah? I wondered if they meant the new age woman who had a medicine wheel tattooed on her right forearm, a medicine wheel tattooed on the left side of her chest and Celtic writing tattooed on her forearm, with Chinese characters tattooed on her left forearm, and wearing tight fitting stretchy pants that were slowly turning grayish-white on the knees and rear? She had met Lisa and told her how she had slept with all the shamans who would be presenting at the gathering. When she moved from sitting on Lisa's deer hide I sprayed the hide with some Lysol, after smudging it of course.

"I don't love Sarah," I said. I knew this was my end. The dragon and griffin leapt into the air flapping their wings. I thought if I could fight off any of them it would be the hedgehog, but I couldn't see it. As the two winged animals began to hover, I found the hedgehog as its nose appeared out of some fresh dirt near my foot. Just then a great wind came and caused the dragon to twist and turn in the air. It and the griffin struggled to maintain flight, then surrendered to the wind and crashed to the ground with large thuds. The hedgehog remained in its hole for cover. I was amazed because the wind hadn't touched me.

Again, I wondered, "Am I dead?"

Then over my right should there came a bright light. In the light was a shadow. As the shadow came closer it took the shape of a bird. The light flickered for a moment and standing there was a large hawk. Its size was three times the size of the dragon.

"Leave!" the hawk said with a strong command. The dragon and griffin hissed and took flight and disappeared into the darkness. I looked down at my feet and the little hedgehog's nose disappeared. They all left.

"Thank you, thank you," I said.

"Go home now," said the hawk.

"I didn't call you," I said.

"The one who loves you called me and asked me to help you. This one joins the requests of your relatives. There are many who ask for help for you," said the hawk.

"But Lisa isn't..."

"She loves you and you don't know how much that means here, in this reality," said the hawk. With that he jumped into the air and took flight, saying, "It isn't the color, or the size of the source, it is the belief and love that counts. Go home now to your world." With that, the hawk disappeared.

I woke up. Twice in one morning.

Biographies

Susan Deer Cloud, a Catskill Mountain Indian, is the recipient of an NEA Literature Fellowship, two New York State Foundation for the Arts Poetry Fellowships, and an Elizabeth George Foundation Grant. Published in numerous literary journals and anthologies, some of her books are *Hunger Moon*, *Fox Mountain*, *Braiding Starlight*, *Car Stealer* and *The Last Ceremony*. She also edits ongoing Native anthology *I Was Indian (Before Being Indian Was Cool)* and the *Re-Matriation Chapbook Series of Indigenous Poetry*. A long haired rover, Deer Cloud loves wandering with fiery dreamers and feral cats whose eyes mirror the Van Gogh nights.

Phyllis Fast, Koyukon Athabascan, was born in Anchorage Alaska. Her academic degrees include a PhD from Harvard (1998). She has written numerous nonfiction publications, including one nonfiction book *(Northern Athabascan Survival: Women, Community and the Future)* for which she received the 2000 North American Indian Prose Award. In 2006, she received the Alaska Native Writer on the Environment award for "Of Tadpoles and Spruce Pitch." After a long career in teaching at the University of Alaska, she retired as Professor Emerita (2014) and is now focusing on painting and writing fiction.

Dean K. Hutchins is of Cherokee ancestry and grew up in New York. He is a systems engineer and internationally known computer methodologist. He has been published in *Talking Stick, Native Realities, Garbaj,* and was a contributing author to *Unraveling the Spreading Cloth of Time.* He has appeared at the People's Poetry Gathering, the American Museum of Natural History, the Museum of the American Indian, the Native American Video Cultural Festival, The Nuyorican Poets Café, The American Indian Community House, QPTV, and on Pacifica Radio. He currently serves as Chairman of the Nuyagi Keetoowah Society and lives in Fairfax County, Virginia.

Amy Krout-Horn has lived in two worlds: the world of the sighted and the world of the blind. She has been a writer in both of them. She is the co-author of TRANSCENDENCE, which won the 2012 National Indie Excellence Award, and MY FATHER'S BLOOD, an autobiographical novel. Her latest novel, DANCING IN CONCRETE MOCCASINS, will be released in 2016. Amy lives and writes with her life-partner, Gabriel Horn, on Coquina Key, near the Gulf of Mexico.

Gabriel Horn – White Deer of Autumn – Indigenous: selected Who's Who Among America's Teachers; presented the University of South Florida's Alumni Award for Professional Achievement; Professor Emeritus, St. Petersburg

College; co-authored with his life companion, Amy Krout-Horn, TRANSCENDENCE, the National INDIE Excellence Book Award for Visionary Fiction; author of the new Indigenous eco novel, MOTHERLESS. Other works: *The Book of Ceremonies; Native Heart; Contemplations of a Primal Mind;* children, The Native People / Native Ways series; *The Great Change; Ceremony – in the Circle of Life.* Godson of Princess Red Wing, nephew of Metacomet, and Nippawanock. Outspoken defender of the natural world.

Denise Low, 2nd Kansas Poet Laureate, is award-winning author of 25 books, including *Jackalope*, short fiction, and *Mélange Block*, poetry (Red Mountain Press). Her memoir *The Turtle's Beating Heart* is forthcoming from the University of Nebraska Press. Low is past board president of the Associated Writers and Writing Programs. Her MFA is from Wichita St. Univ. and PhD is from the Univ. of Kansas. She has British Isles, German, and Lenape/Munsee heritage.www.deniselow.net

Sean Milanovich is a PhD student at the University California Riverside within the History Department. Sean's research focuses on Southern California Indian history. He works at the Riverside Metropolitan Museum as Associate Curator of Anthropology. Milanovich is a member of the Agua Caliente Band of Cahuilla Indians.

MariJo Moore (Cherokee/Irish/Dutch) is an author/editor/anthologist/psychic/medium and workshop facilitator. The author of over twenty books including *A Book of Ceremonies and Spiritual Energies Thereof, The Diamond Doorknob, When the Dead Dream, Red Woman With Backward Eyes and Other Stories, The Boy With a Tree Growing from His Ear and Other Stories, Crow Quotes,* and *Bear Quotes.* She is also editor of several anthologies including *Unraveling the Spreading Cloth of Time Indigenous Thoughts Concerning the Universe.* She resides in the mountains of western NC. www.marijomoore.com

Dr Dawn Karima Pettigrew is a Native American Music Award Winner for her CD THE DESIRE OF NATIONS and an Indigenous Artist Activist Award Winner. Nominated for an Indigenous Music Award for her CD, THE STARS OF HEAVEN and for her radio program, A CONVERSATION WITH DAWN KARIMA, she is the author of two novels, THE WAY WE MAKE SENSE, a finalist for the Native American First Book Award and THE MARRIAGE OF SAINTS, a finalist for the New Mexico Book Award. SINGING OF THE STARS is her newly released volume of poetry.

Evan Pritchard, "Abachbahametch" ("Chipmunk") of Mi'kmaq and Celtic descent, is the author of *Bird Medicine: The Sacred Power of Bird Shamanism* (Inner Traditions 2013), *No Word*

For Time, Native American Stories of the Sacred, Native New Yorkers. His poetry book *Greetings from Mawenawasic Foothills*, 2014) features a foreword by legendary Mohawk poet Susan Deer Cloud. He is the founder and director of the Center for Algonquin Culture, which is also creating a series of books of words and phrases in Algonquian languages. He has worked with countless elders to help preserve the ancient history of North America, notably the late William Commanda. www.algonquinculture.org.

Lois Red Elk. First and foremost I am a D/Lakota Culturalist. Preserving my culture from stereotyping led me to films, television, stage and radio. I have been a technical advisor, actor, writer, producer, and have worked with all the major studios in Los Angeles. After returning to my homelands, I developed and taught cultural topics for Fort Peck Community College where I'm an adjunct professor. I've written one chapbook and three poetry books. *Our Blood Remembers* and *Why I Return to Makoce* both from Many Voices Press won, best non-fiction, 2012 and best poetry, 2015 from Wordcraft Circle of Native Writers and Storytellers.

Jim Stevens is a poet, musician and photographer of Seneca and German ancestry. He was born in Milwaukee and grew up among the spirit hills of southeastern Wisconsin's kettle moraine region. He lived for many years in Madison (where this story takes place) and presently lives in northern Wisconsin. *Book of Big Dog Town*, his most recent collection of poetry and prose was published in 2013.

Clifford Trafzer is Distinguished Professor of History and Rupert Costo Chair in American Indian Affairs at the University of California, Riverside. Areas of specialization: Native American Social-Cultural History; American West; Oral Traditions; Public History. Raised in Arizona, he was born to parents of Wyandot Indian and German blood. He is the author of numerous books including *As Long As The Grass Shall Grow and Rivers Flow*: *A History of Native Americans and Kit Carson Campaign*: *The Last Great Navajo War* His work also appeared in *Unraveling the Spreading Cloth of Time: Indigenous Thoughts Concerning the Universe.*

William S. Yellow Robe, Jr. (Assiniboine/Nakoda) is from the Fort Peck Indian reservation located in northeastern Montana. He is an Adjunct Faculty in the English Department at the University of Maine and is a Faculty Affiliate in the Creative Writing department at the University of Montana. His books include two anthologies of his work: *Grandchildren of the Buffalo Soldiers and Other Untold Stories*, a collection of full-length plays, and *Where the Pavement Ends: New Native Drama*, a collection of his one-act plays. He is published in poetry, short fiction, and drama/plays.

Made in the USA
Charleston, SC
11 March 2016